Scaling Up: A Research Agenda For Software Engineering

Computer Science and Technology Board
Commission on Physical Sciences, Mathematics, and Resources
National Research Council

NATIONAL ACADEMY PRESS
Washington, D.C.   1989

NOTICE: The project that is the subject of this report was approved by the Governing Board of the National Research Council, whose members are drawn from the councils of the National Academy of Sciences, the National Academy of Engineering, and the Institute of Medicine. The members of the committee responsible for the report were chosen for their special competences and with regard for appropriate balance.

This report has been reviewed by a group other than the authors according to procedures approved by a Report Review Committee consisting of members of the National Academy of Sciences, the National Academy of Engineering, and the Institute of Medicine.

The National Academy of Sciences is a private, nonprofit, self-perpetuating society of distinguished scholars engaged in scientific and engineering research, dedicated to the furtherance of science and technology and to their use for the general welfare. Upon the authority of the charter granted to it by the Congress in 1863, the Academy has a mandate that requires it to advise the federal government on scientific and technical matters. Dr. Frank Press is president of the National Academy of Sciences.

The National Academy of Engineering was established in 1964, under the charter of the National Academy of Sciences, as a parallel organization of outstanding engineers. It is autonomous in its administration and in the selection of its members, sharing with the National Academy of Sciences the responsibility for advising the federal government. The National Academy of Engineering also sponsors engineering programs aimed at meeting national needs, encourages education and research, and recognizes the superior achievements of engineers. Dr. Robert M. White is president of the National Academy of Engineering.

The Institute of Medicine was established in 1970 by the National Academy of Sciences to secure the services of eminent members of appropriate professions in the examination of policy matters pertaining to the health of the public. The Institute acts under the responsibility given to the National Academy of Sciences by its congressional charter to be an adviser to the federal government and, upon its own initiative, to identify issues of medical care, research, and education. Dr. Samuel O. Thier is president of the Institute of Medicine.

The National Research Council was organized by the National Academy of Sciences in 1916 to associate the broad community of science and technology with the Academy's purposes of furthering knowledge and advising the federal government. Functioning in accordance with general policies determined by the Academy, the Council has become the principal operating agency of both the National Academy of Sciences and the National Academy of Engineering in providing services to the government, the public, and the scientific and engineering communities. The Council is administered jointly by both Academies and the Institute of Medicine. Dr. Frank Press and Dr. Robert M. White are chairman and vice chairman, respectively, of the National Research Council.

Support for this project was provided by the following organizations and agencies: Control Data Corporation, Cray Research, Inc., the Defense Advanced Research Projects Agency (Grant No. N00014-87-J-1110), Digital Equipment Corporation, the Department of Energy (Contract No. DE-FG05-87ER25029), Hewlett Packard, IBM Corporation, the National Aeronautics and Space Administration (Grant No. CDA-860535), the National Science Foundation (Grant No. CDA-860535), and the Office of Naval Research (Grant No. N00014-87-J-1110).

Library of Congress Catalog Card No. 89-63272
International Standard Book Number 0-309-04131-7

Available from:
National Academy Press
2101 Constitution Avenue, NW
Washington, DC 20418

S039
Printed in the United States of America

First Printing, October 1989
Second Printing, June 1990

COMPUTER SCIENCE AND TECHNOLOGY BOARD

JOSEPH F. TRAUB, Columbia University, *Chairman*
JOHN SEELY BROWN, Xerox Corporation
MICHAEL L. DERTOUZOS, Massachusetts Institute of Technology
SAMUEL H. FULLER, Digital Equipment Corporation
JAMES FREEMAN GILBERT, University of California at San Diego
WILLIAM A. GODDARD III, California Institute of Technology
JOHN E. HOPCROFT, Cornell University
ROBERT E. KAHN, Corporation for National Research Initiatives
SIDNEY KARIN, General Atomics
LEONARD KLEINROCK, University of California at Los Angeles
DAVID J. KUCK, University of Illinois at Urbana-Champaign
ROBERT LANGRIDGE, University of California at San Francisco
ROBERT W. LUCKY, AT&T Bell Laboratories
RAJ REDDY, Carnegie Mellon University
MARY SHAW, Carnegie Mellon University
WILLIAM J. SPENCER, Xerox Corporation
IVAN E. SUTHERLAND, Sutherland, Sproull & Associates
VICTOR VYSSOTSKY, Digital Equipment Corporation
SHMUEL WINOGRAD, IBM T. J. Watson Research Center
IRVING WLADAWSKY-BERGER, IBM Corporation

MARJORY S. BLUMENTHAL, Staff Director
DAMIAN M. SACCOCIO, Staff Officer
MARGARET A. KNEMEYER, Staff Associate
C. K. GUNSALUS, Staff Consultant
DONNA F. ALLEN, Administrative Secretary
CATHERINE A. SPARKS, Secretary

COMMISSION ON PHYSICAL SCIENCES, MATHEMATICS, AND RESOURCES

NORMAN HACKERMAN, Robert A. Welch Foundation, *Chairman*
ROBERT C. BEARDSLEY, Woods Hole Oceanographic Institution
B. CLARK BURCHFIEL, Massachusetts Institute of Technology
GEORGE F. CARRIER, Harvard University
RALPH J. CICERONE, National Center for Atmospheric Research
HERBERT D. DOAN, The Dow Chemical Company (retired)
PETER S. EAGLESON, Massachusetts Institute of Technology
DEAN E. EASTMAN, IBM T. J. Watson Research Center
MARYE ANNE FOX, University of Texas
GERHART FRIEDLANDER, Brookhaven National Laboratory
LAWRENCE W. FUNKHOUSER, Chevron Corporation (retired)
PHILLIP A. GRIFFITHS, Duke University
NEAL F. LANE, Rice University
CHRISTOPHER F. McKEE, University of California at Berkeley
RICHARD S. NICHOLSON, American Association for the Advancement of Science
JACK E. OLIVER, Cornell University
JEREMIAH P. OSTRIKER, Princeton University Observatory
PHILIP A. PALMER, E.I. du Pont de Nemours & Company
FRANK L. PARKER, Vanderbilt University
DENIS J. PRAGER, MacArthur Foundation
DAVID M. RAUP, University of Colorado
ROY F. SCHWITTERS, Superconducting Super Collider Laboratory
LARRY L. SMARR, University of Illinois at Urbana-Champaign
KARL K. TUREKIAN, Yale University

MYRON F. UMAN, Acting Executive Director
ROBERT M. SIMON, Acting Associate Executive Director

Preface

How to produce software of sufficient quality and in sufficient quantity to meet national needs is a problem that has been festering for some time and is getting worse. Of particular concern is the need to facilitate the development of software for large and complex systems, on which the world is becoming critically dependent. This problem has concerned the National Research Council's Computer Science and Technology Board (CSTB) since its inception in 1986.

On February 13-15, 1989, in Austin, Texas, the CSTB sponsored a two-and-one-half-day workshop on complex software systems research needs. A diverse group of software engineers, representing a range of industry perspectives and the academic community, participated (Appendix A). The workshop was chaired by Victor Vyssotsky of Digital Equipment Corporation, and the steering committee included Laszlo Belady of Microelectronics and Computer Technology Corporation (MCC), Mary Shaw of Carnegie Mellon University, and Shmuel Winograd of IBM Corporation's T. J. Watson Research Center.

The CSTB workshop took as a starting point the notion that large and growing opportunity costs are resulting from the inability to produce sophisticated, reliable software in a timely manner. Its objective was to identify directions for software engineering research and potential mechanisms to improve the way software engineering research builds from and contributes to practice in the field. Consequently, workshop discussions focused on characterizing impediments perceived by software engineers, promising research directions, and options for improving the interplay between software engineering research and practice.

This report summarizes the deliberations of workshop participants, focusing on directions for research. Included in Appendix B are brief position statements contributed by individual participants. The report is aimed at leaders in the academic and corporate research community who should be concerned about large-system software engineering. It is also directed to government funders of software engineering research, who control key levers of change.

                                          Joseph F. Traub, *Chairman*
                                    Computer Science and Technology Board

Contents

1 INTRODUCTION AND SUMMARY 1
2 PERSPECTIVE 7
3 ENGINEERING PRACTICE 15
4 RESEARCH MODES 19
5 CONCLUSIONS 23
   BIBLIOGRAPHY 25

APPENDIXES

A WORKSHOP PARTICIPANTS 31
B POSITION STATEMENTS 32

1
Introduction and Summary

Business, government, and technical endeavors ranging from financial transactions to space missions increasingly require complex software systems to function. The complexity of the software arises from stringent requirements (e.g., for reliability in performance and integrity of the data used), the need to support a range of interactions with the environment in real time, and/or certain structural features (see Table 1.1). These attributes make software difficult to produce and often require large-scale projects involving the efforts of several hundred—even a few thousand—programmers, software engineers, applications experts, and others working for one year or more. The difficulty of developing complex software systems tends to force delays in the implementation of new applications, compromises in what those applications can do, and uncertainties about their reliability. (See Box for a more detailed characterization of the problem.) As a result, there is a perception in the field, especially in industry, that opportunity costs are large and growing.

How can this situation be improved? The problem has resisted the efforts of many talented individuals over many years. Some degree of resistance to change is inevitable, reflecting the inertia that comes from the large and cumulative investment that companies have made in their software development processes, but CSTB workshop participants expressed a widely shared frustration that options circulating within the software engineering community fall short of what is needed (or fall on deaf ears). Solutions suggested in the past have ranged from ways to improve tools used by software developers to ways to improve the management of software development teams; they have often been couched as options for improving productivity in software development, itself a slippery and many-sided concept.

AGENDA FOR SOFTWARE ENGINEERING RESEARCH

Directions for Change

Acknowledging those suggestions and accepting that there may be no "silver bullet" in this area (Brooks, 1986), CSTB workshop participants reached the consensus that progress will be made if the vast array of existing and emerging knowledge can be codified, unified, distributed, and extended more systematically. Software requirements

TABLE 1.1 Observations on Complex Systems

What makes complex systems complex? Is complexity inherent when software is the focal point of the system? How can we characterize the complexity of software systems? Can we identify avoidable and unavoidable kinds of complexity? Looking at systems from a broad perspective, we see several ways in which they may be complex:

Structure Subsystems, modules, macros, down to statements and expressions

Behavior Observable activity of a system

>**Function** Transformations on components of the state
>**Process** Flow of control
>**Reactivity** Events to which the system must respond
>**Timing** Constraints on response times

State Persistent and transient data with associated consistency and correctness invariants

Application Requirements from the context in which system will be used

>**Recovery** of state and continuation of reactivity
>**Security** of state from destruction or unwanted inspection
>**Safety** from catastrophic external or internal events
>**Interfaces** with users and other systems
>**Operations** that maintain the state and continuity of the system

Development environment People and processes producing the code

>**Design and implementation**
>**Documentation and training**
>**Verification, validation, and certification**

SOURCE: Adapted from "Complexity, Multiple Paradigms, and Analysis," position statement by Susan L. Gerhart, Appendix B.

for large and complex systems have been outrunning understanding of their fundamental principles, and software development practices have not filled that gap. Further, the shared framework of existing knowledge has not grown commensurately with advances made by individual practitioners. Codification of existing knowledge would help to make the process of developing routine software (which is what most software is) more routine, thereby saving time and money. It is essential for progress in the reuse of knowledge. A strategy for dissemination of codified knowlege should build on the concept of software engineering handbooks.

Computer Science and Technology Board workshop participants agreed that software engineering research can contribute to the improvement of practice if the research community broadens its view of what constitutes good research (and amends its reward structure accordingly). In particular, researchers need to look to practice to find good research problems, validating results against the needs of practice as well as against more abstract standards. The problems experienced by practitioners are serious and pressing, and they call for innovative solutions. The promise of fruitful interactions between researchers and practitioners should not have to founder because of cultural differences between the two groups.

The CSTB workshop underscored the need for both software engineering researchers and practitioners to accept a more realistic view of the problem. Many of the problems experienced today reflect implicit assumptions that the flow from software system concept to implementation is smoother and more orderly than it is, as well as implicit assumptions that a development process involving project teams is subject to the degree and kind of control that might be found if a single individual were responsible for the software. A

CHARACTERIZING THE PROBLEM: OBSERVATIONS FROM THE FIELD

There are few human endeavors that are as difficult to grasp as a complex program or set of programs. The relations, processes, and purposes of the elements of a program are difficult to describe and thus difficult to use as construction elements. Creating tools, methods, or magic to solve these difficulties is extremely hard.

The worst problem is not cost; it's not unreliability; it's not schedule slips. Rather, it's the fact that in the near future we won't be able to produce requisite software *at all*!

Both industry and government do not take management actions which recognize the industry's inability to efficiently develop large software packages.

The typical system development life cycle is so long that only a few people will have the opportunity to learn by repetition during a typical career.

The state of practice in software development and maintenance is far behind the state of [the] art.

Even when more 'modern' software development techniques and technologies are widespread, new and unanticipated requirements for *'ities'* (e.g., usability, installability, reliability, integrity, security, recoverability, reconfigurability, serviceability, etc.) which are not yet taught in software engineering, are not yet part of the methodology being used, and are not yet 'parameters' to the code generator will necessitate rediscovery and rework of our complex systems.

[My company's] most significant software problem is duplication of effort; we often write several times what appears to be essentially the same software.

All problems pale against the issue of chasing the leading edge of technology. . . . For instance, our state-of-the-practice can finally handle serial, monolithic systems quite well but our challenge is distributed, parallel, asynchronous applications for which we have little or no practical engineering principles.

Industry does not collaborate effectively with the research community in creating the next generation of software capability and software production technology.

A key motivator for software tools and programmer education in the 1990s will be software evolved over decades from several thousand line, sequential programming systems into multi-million line, multi-tasking complex systems.

Without clear understanding of design, developing and teaching skills and developing better tools will continue to be happenstance.

What we call the problem of requirements generation is actually a poverty of tools, techniques, and language to assist business experts and computer scientists in collaborating on a process of transformation which adequately exploits the knowledge of all.

The worst problem I must contend with is the inability of the software buyer, user, and builder to write a blueprint which quickly leads to a low-cost, correct product.

A most serious problem . . . is . . . cost and schedule increases due to changing user requirements.

Too often funders, customers, and managers are willing to be 'low balled' on effort estimation. The lack of appreciation for up-front capitalization in the software industry with consequential failures points to a serious problem confronting us.

Non-programmers dominate modern computer use. . . . Computer users are interested in results, not in programming; software must reflect this.

Users of software have reliability and economic (speed, space, cost) constraints that are of little interest to the computer scientist; the computer scientist has solutions which, when properly engineered, could greatly enhance products.

Technology to enable satisfaction of capability requirements, such as for high assurance, deadline guarantees, and high adaptability is not being provided, despite need.

We need a true pragmatic test engineering discipline. Today it is a truism that we test until out of money and time, not because we've achieved results.

There is a rigorous science, just waiting to be recognized and developed, which encompasses the whole of 'the software problem,' as defined, including the hardware, software, languages, devices, logic, data, knowledge, users, uses, and effectiveness, etc. for end-users, providers, enablers, commissioners, and sponsors, alike.

SOURCE: Quotations from position statements prepared before workshop (Appendix B).

TABLE 1.2 Agenda for Software Engineering Research

	Recommended Actions	
	Short Term (1-5 years)	Long Term (5-10 years)
Perspective	Portray systems realistically • View systems as systems • Recognize change as intrinsic Study and preserve software artifacts	Research a unifying model for software development--for matching programming languages to applications domains and design phases Strengthen mathematical and scientific foundations
Engineering practice	Codify software engineering knowledge for dissemination and reuse Develop software engineering handbooks	Automate handbook knowledge, access, and reuse--and make development of routine software more routine Nurture collaboration among system developers and between developers and users
Research modes	Foster practitioner and researcher interactions	Legitimize academic exploration of large software systems in situ Glean insights from behavioral and managerial sciences Develop additional research directions and paradigms--encourage recognition of review studies, contributions to handbooks

clearer understanding of the realities of software development can lead to improvements in any of several ways. For example, it may facilitate the identification of valuable tools that do not now exist, or it may facilitate the identification of fundamental flaws in the software development process itself. A more realistic view will also make clear the extent to which problems are technical or are amenable to technical solutions.

Specific Short- and Long-Term Actions

Improving the development of complex software systems requires a series of long-term (5 to 10 years or more) and short-term (1 to 5 years) measures. The CSTB workshop reached consensus on several directions for change in software engineering research, which fall into three interconnected areas: (1) perspective, (2) engineering practice, and (3) modes of research (see Table 1.2). These improvements are outlined below and discussed in greater detail in the body of the report. Carried out together, they will bring to software engineering strengths found in traditional engineering disciplines, notably the effective reuse of shared knowledge and a working distinction between routine and innovative design. Some of these directions have been advanced before; others are more novel. CSTB workshop participants shared the hope that this new presentation and the consensus it represents will help to catalyze much-needed changes.

Perspective

Portray the Software Development Process More Realistically. Changes in attitude take time to achieve, but the time is right to push for better models of the software development process in research, teaching, and management. Today's systems are conglomerate wholes, not mere collections of parts, and change is intrinsic in such systems. A new approach to software design that accounts for system evolution and that aggressively links software development and application expertise could provide a basis for advances in practice. A sampling of the software engineering leadership, CSTB workshop participants noted that outmoded models lead to unrealistic expectations among developers or managers; such models contribute to delay and diminish quality by engendering inappropriately tight schedules and complicating the process of mid-course corrections. Further, new attitudes are prerequisite to other steps being satisfactorily developed and implemented.

Study and Preserve Software Artifacts. A better understanding of the process of system development would provide useful perspectives and insights for today's researchers and practitioners. Because such an understanding must be built on the study of actual systems, itself a dynamic process, an ongoing mechanism for studying innovative systems now in existence should be established. Looking at snapshots of a system may be easy, but it does not provide sufficient information to permit realistic portrayal of the software development process. CSTB workshop participants urged efforts to preserve and study software artifacts and their development processes in the hope that understanding their structure and properties would contribute to the development of better experiments, tools, and software development methods.

Develop Unifying Models and Strengthen Mathematical and Scientific Foundations. Long-term efforts that will enhance research and education include developing unifying models for system development and associated languages, which are the basic units of the software development process. A comprehensive and unifying view of models and languages would be a valuable analytical device that could help researchers develop new tools and techniques to enhance the structure and development of large software systems. Also, strengthening the mathematical and scientific foundations of software development will help software engineers to improve the quality of software systems and to produce them more systematically. For example, the degree of rigor in software design and analysis (including testing and other verification and validation methods) should be increased.

Engineering Practice

Codify and Disseminate Software Engineering Knowledge. Codification of knowledge can help move the practice of software engineering from a craft toward a science. Broad dissemination of software engineering insights and techniques that are known now will save time by making much useful information broadly and conveniently available, thus reducing duplication of effort and enhancing software development productivity. In particular, it will help make development of routine software more routine. This dissemination can be achieved through software engineering handbooks, providing for software engineers the reference assistance other types of engineers have benefited from for decades. And the handbooks need not be limited to conventional book form; they can be developed and accessed in electronic formats. Over the long term, new technologies (e.g., advanced networking and data base systems) will enhance the delivery and use of what should be shared knowledge, but the codification and dissemination process should be launched now.

Nurture Collaboration Among System Developers and Between Developers and Users. The development of large software systems involves many people acting in concert. Progress is especially needed to facilitate communication and cooperation between software developers and applications experts and other end-users; this is a long-term issue. Because software engineers have an incomplete understanding of the process of collaboration, tools to support software development are not optimal. Support for research into and development and use of computer-supported tools for collaborative work would improve the software development process.

Research Modes

Foster Practitioner and Researcher Interaction and Legitimize Academic Exploration of Large Software Systems. Academic researchers lack access to large complex software systems, which are developed and used primarily in commercial and defense-related industries. As a result, these researchers have encountered difficulty in teaching large-system topics and in identifying good basic research problems related to large-system development. New ways should be explored to facilitate interaction between software engineers in academia and industry, including expediting academic exploration of large systems, promoting outlets for information that would reach both academic and corporate researchers, and augmenting current teaching of large-system concepts. Legitimizing the study of large systems (and their development) in situ would be a major step in the right direction.

Glean Insights from Behavioral and Managerial Science. Collaboration by software engineering researchers with other types of researchers, including those from the behavioral and management sciences, may lead to insights into the people-driven process of software system development. Although project management and administration are only a part of the complex system problem, insights from other disciplines may enhance the planning, management, and timeliness of system projects, which have resisted efforts from within the software engineering field.

Develop New Research Paradigms. The field would benefit from such new efforts as review and synthesis studies, case studies, and comparative analyses, which have not made the same mark on software engineering as on other fields, because such studies would help to advance the codification and reuse of knowledge. Similarly, researchers should get credit for contributions to the electronic handbooks discussed above.

ORGANIZATION AND CONTENT OF THIS REPORT

The remainder of this report of the CSTB Workshop on Complex Software Systems examines each research agenda item in turn. Chapter 2 covers the area of perspective, Chapter 3 discusses engineering practice, and Chapter 4 addresses research modes. Chapter 5 presents brief conclusions and a call to action. A bibliography is given in a final chapter. Appendix A lists workshop participants, and Appendix B contains position statements prepared by individual participants in the workshop.

Determining the details of implementing the measures outlined below was beyond the scope of the CSTB workshop. It is clear, however, that implementation of the recommended measures will hinge on funding for corresponding research projects and other incentives. Selected implementation issues will be addressed in follow-up work by the CSTB.

2
Perspective

The software research community has not kept up with the development of complex software systems in industry and government, while in the field, managers concerned with procuring software systems often evince idealized and unrealistic views of how software is developed. A critical reality in the field that is insufficiently appreciated by academic researchers and systems purchasers is the extent to which existing systems tie up resources. So-called system maintenance, discussed below, may constitute up to 75 percent of a system's cost over its lifetime. The high cost of maintenance diminishes the amount of money available to replace existing systems, and it lengthens the payback period for investment in new system development. It makes designing for a system's entire life cycle imperative, but such design is rarely if ever achieved. CSTB workshop participants agreed that to progress in system development, it is time to portray systems realistically by (1) viewing software systems as systems—which has implications for optimal system design, (2) recognizing that change is intrinsic in large systems, and (3) striving for a better and more timely blending of software engineering and applications expertise (see discussions headed "Build a Unifying Model," p. 10, and "Nurture Collaboration," p. 17).[1] They also agreed that a more rigorous use of mathematical techniques can help researchers to manage and diminish complexity.

SHORT-TERM ACTIONS

Portray Systems Realistically

View Systems as Systems, not as Collections of Parts

While the computer field has helped to popularize the word "systems" and the concept of systems, it is ironic that information systems developers have not developed formal mechanisms to understand systems and the interrelationships among system components. Software engineering researchers have been unable to provide effective guidance to practitioners regarding the process of system definition and the concomitant implementation of functional elements. Progress in developing software systems requires a fundamental appreciation that those systems are more than just a collection of parts and that software is embedded in larger systems with a variety of physical components;

design of such systems must deal with both of these issues. Design of software systems must also take into account the fact that the whole system includes people as well as hardware, software, and a wide variety of material elements.

Recognize Change as Intrinsic in Large Systems

Software projects are increasingly likely to be built on top of an existing, installed base of code rather than built anew. As that installed base of software grows over time, software systems that might or might not have been designed to endure have been patched, modified, and "maintained," transforming them greatly from their original designs and functions (Belady and Lehman, 1985). Two factors are at work here: The first is that systems are often not well-enough designed to begin with, and the second is that user needs change over time—new requirements arise, and existing systems must be adapted to accommodate them. But commonly used conceptualizations, such as the "waterfall model" or even the "spiral model," assume a more sure-footed progression from requirement specification to design to coding to testing and to delivery of software than is realistic (Royce, 1970; Boehm, 1988). Given that 40 to 60 percent or more of the effort in the development of complex software systems goes into maintaining—i.e., changing—such systems (Boehm, 1981), the design and development processes could be made more efficient if the reality of change were accepted explicitly.

Sustaining the usefulness of software systems differs from the care of other assets because it entails two distinct activities: (1) corrective and preventive maintenance, which includes the repair of latent defects and technological wear and tear, and (2) enhancement, which normally introduces major transformations not only in the form but also in the functions and objectives of the software. Enhancement activities have been observed to constitute perhaps 75 percent of the total maintenance effort.[2]

The degree and impact of change is analogous to the evolution of an urban neighborhood: Over time, old and obsolete buildings are torn down, the supply of utilities changes in both quality and delivery aspects, and transportation routes and media change. As new needs, wants, and capabilities emerge, the structure and function of the neighborhood evolve; the neighborhood is not thrown out wholesale and replaced because doing so would be far too costly. As with changes in neighborhoods, changes in software are not always improvements; software systems suffer from the tension between providing for functional flexibility and assuring structural integrity of the system.

Software developers in industry and government are increasingly aware that change occurs from the earliest design stages as initial expressions of customer requirements are refined. Managing this change involves managing a mix of old code (typically with inadequate documentation of original specifications as well as modifications made over time), new programmers, and new technology. The process is ad hoc, and the problem grows over time; the larger the installed base of code, the more formidable the problem. The problem is aggravated where management decisions, including contracting decisions, keep developers and maintainers separate.

Ideally, system designers leave hooks for the changes they can anticipate, but problems arise from major changes that result from changed circumstances or goals. Also, schedule and process pressures often militate against providing for functional flexibility and future changes. Further, the current generation of computer-aided tools for software engineers concentrates on development activities and generally neglects maintenance. As a result, supporting information for new code and the tools to exploit it are not carried forward from development to maintenance. More seriously, these tools do not accommodate large bodies of code developed without using the tools, although some progress is being made in the necessary restructuring of programs to accommodate computer-aided tools.

Just as change, per se, should be accepted as a basic factor in most large, complex systems, designing for change should become a fundamental body of knowledge and skill. The very notion of maintenance as an activity separate from the creation process seems to legitimize high costs, poor support, and poorly managed redesign. Eliminating this notion via a move toward designing and building systems in anticipation of change would help to increase the engineering control over post-release modification. Since software reflects both system specifications and design decisions, changing either element will indirectly produce changes in the code. One possibility is to strive for designing systems that are more modular or easier to replace as needs change.

Note that the issue of determining what the software shall do (the "requirements definition") is much broader than software engineering practices today would suggest; this perceptual difference contributes to the maintenance problem. What is needed is a thorough investigation, analysis, and synthesis of what the combined functions will, or should, be of the automated and non-automated (human, business, or physical) elements of the system, including all "think flows," work flows, information flows, and other functionalities. A total systems approach, as discussed above, would be involved, with a heavy emphasis on the conceptualization of the functional role of both the automated parts and the fully combined systems, allowing for reengineering to accommodate or exploit the changes that are made possible by introduction of the automated system.

Understanding the reasons for change and the costs, impacts, and methods of change could lead to more control of a major part of software development costs. Creating mechanisms that allow for change and that make systems robust while undergoing change will help to reduce opportunity costs in system development and deployment. Part of what is needed is a change in attitude. But for the long term, a theory of software systems is needed that will build on empirical study of software system applications.

Study and Preserve Software Artifacts: Learn From Real Systems Past and Present

Although systems developers work with an evolving set of goals and technologies, they can still learn valuable lessons from existing systems, lessons about what led to success or failure and what triggered incremental or major advances. The history of computing is replete with instances in which identifying the intellectual origins of key developments is difficult or impossible because most advances, in their time, were not thought of as intellectual issues but instead were treated as particular solutions to the problems of the day. Most software specialists would be hard put to name "seven wonders of the software systems world" or to state why those wonders are noteworthy.[3] Meanwhile, the artifacts of such systems are disappearing every day as older equipment and systems are replaced with newer ones, as projects end, and as new applications emerge. Because almost all large software systems have been built in corporate or government settings where obsolete systems are eventually replaced, and because those systems have received little academic attention, useful information may be vanishing.

A concerted effort is needed to study (and in some cases preserve) systems and to develop a process for the systematic examination of contemporary and new systems as they arise. Immediate archival of major software artifacts, together with the software tools needed to examine them, or even to experiment with them, would enable both contemporary and future study. Systematic study of those systems would facilitate understanding of the ontology of architecture and system components, provide a basis for measuring what goes on in software development, and support the construction of better program generators.

Studies of contemporary systems would provide an understanding of the characteristics of software developed under present techniques. Such an effort would examine software entities such as requirements documentation, design representation, and testing and support tools, in addition to the actual source code itself, which has traditionally been the focus of measurement. Better mechanisms that provide quantifiable measures of requirements, design, and testing aspects must be developed in order to understand the quality baseline that exists today. Existing mechanisms for measuring source code must be put to more widespread use to better assess their utility and to refine them (Bowen et al., 1985; McCabe, 1976). In addition, variations in quality need to be traced to their sources to understand how to control and improve the process. Thus this effort should encompass less successful as well as exemplary artifacts, if only to show how poor design affects maintainability. The examination of artifacts should be combined with directed interviews of the practitioners (and system users) and observation of the process to correlate development practices with resulting product quality.

Having quantifiable measurements would enable new, innovative development methods and practices to be evaluated for their impact on product quality. However, as the software industry evolves, so too must the measurement techniques. For example, if new means of representing requirements and design are put into practice, the measurement techniques must be updated to accommodate these new representations. In addition, efforts to automate measurement can be improved if researchers consider measurability as an objective when developing new development methods and design representations.

Such measurement and research cannot take place in the laboratory due to the size of the actual systems being developed (the costs of experiments at this scale are prohibitive), and it is unlikely that small experiments can be extrapolated to apply to large-scale projects. A cooperative effort between government, industry, and academia could provide necessary funding, access to real-world artifacts and practitioners, and the academic research talent required for such an effort. Such a combined effort also would provide an excellent platform for greater collaboration in software engineering research between members of these communities. Designation and funding of one or more responsible entities are needed, and candidates include federal agencies (e.g., the National Science Foundation and the National Institute of Standards and Technology), federally funded research and development centers, or private institutions.

Finally, active discussion of artifacts should be encouraged. A vehicle like the on-line RISKS forum sponsored by the Association for Computing Machinery, which provides a periodic digest and exchange of views among researchers and practitioners on risks associated with computer-based technology, should be established. Also, completed case studies would provide excellent teaching materials.

LONG-TERM ACTIONS

Build a Unifying Model for Software System Development

Shortcomings in software systems often reflect an imperfect fit to the needs of particular users, and in this situation lie the seeds for useful research. The imperfect fit results from the nature of the design and development process: Developers of complex software systems seek to translate the needs of end-users, conveyed in everyday language, into instructions for computer systems. They accomplish this translation by designing systems that can be described at different conceptual levels, ranging from language comprehensible to the intended user (e.g., "plain English" or formal models of the

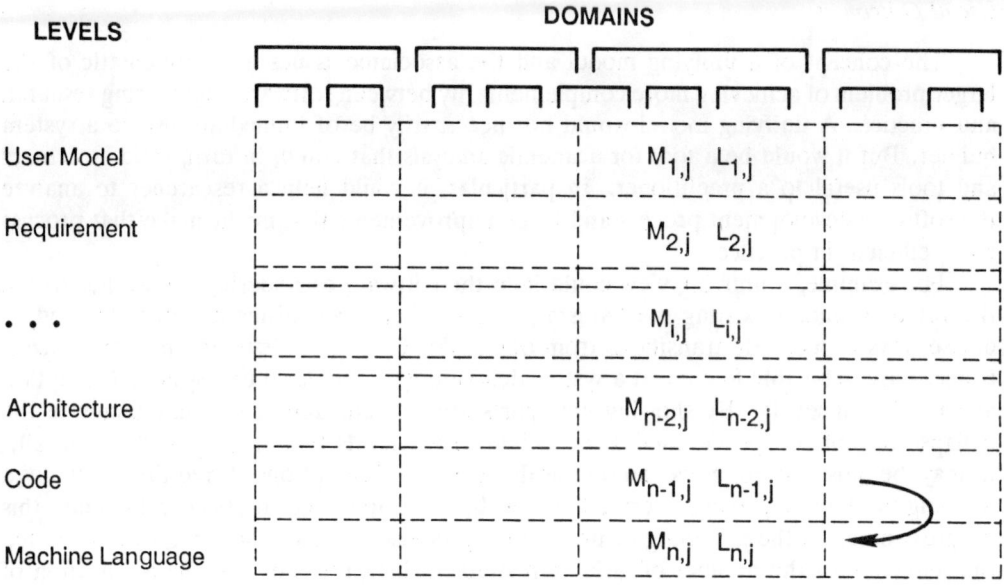

FIGURE 2.1 Illustration of a unifying model for software system design.

application domain) to machine language, which actually drives the computer. Different spheres of activity are referred to by the profession as end-user domains; these include the following:

- scientific computation,
- engineering design,
- modeling and visualization,
- transaction processing, and
- embedded command and control systems.

These domains tend to have different types of abstraction and different language requirements arising from differences in the representations of application information and associated computations. As a result, software developers work with a variety of domain-specific models. During the design process in any domain, key pieces of information or insights tend to be lost or misinterpreted.

How can the process of moving from a domain-specific model to a working piece of software be improved? One approach would be to develop a unifying view of the software design process and the process of abstraction, a view that would define a framework for the task of the complex software system developer. CSTB workshop participants did not reach a consensus on this complicated issue, but to illustrate the point, they began to sketch out the parameters for such a framework (Figure 2.1). For example, a system design can be thought of as a sequence of models, one ($M_{i,j}$) at each level. Different sorts of details and design decisions are dealt with at each level. The model at each level is expressed in a language ($L_{i,j}$). Languages are not necessarily textual or symbolic; they may use graphics or even gestures. Also, languages are not always formally defined.[4] Just as the domains of discourse at each level are different, so are the languages. Finally, the unifying view would distinguish domain-specific models, a multilevel set of appropriate languages (although it is possible that languages may be shared—or largely shared—across domains), abstractions, and interlevel conversion mechanisms.

Useful Outcomes

The concept of a unifying model and the associated issues are emblematic of the larger problem of achieving more complementarity between software engineering research and practice. A unifying model would not necessarily be of immediate use to a system builder. But it would be a tool for academic analysis that could, in turn, yield structures and tools useful to a practitioner. In particular, it could help a researcher to analyze the software development process and forge improvements that might make that process more efficient in practice.

For example, a unifying view could help the software engineering researcher to see the relation among existing mechanisms, to see what mechanisms are missing, and to devise ways to facilitate transitions from one major conceptual level to another (since it is necessary to be able to convert a system description at one level to a system description at an adjacent level).[5] By showing how parts are related, unification may facilitate the collapse of domain-specific models to include fewer levels than at present.[6] Eventually, it may be possible to move automatically from a description of requirements to a working product, bypassing intermediate levels. The modeling process can facilitate this progress much as the modeling of production processes in manufacturing has facilitated the reduction of the number of tasks in manufacturing processes and the application of manufacturing automation. Also useful, as noted above, is better coordination technology, which would support both the modeling and the development processes.

Research Implications

While the theory and nature of program transformation functions, drawing on a body of knowledge about language that crosses levels (sometimes called wide-spectrum language), have already been developed (Balzer, 1985; Partsch and Steinbruggen, 1983; and Smith et al., 1985), the proposed kind of unifying view would also motivate new styles of research independent from those noted above. Relevant current research addresses traditional programming language (although some of this research is in eclipse), computer-supported cooperative work (beyond the mere mechanical aspects—see discussion headed "Nurture Collaboration," p. 17), and efforts to raise the level at which automation can be applied. Also needed are the following:

- Research that would support the development of domain-specific models and corresponding program generators—it is critical to recognize the legitimacy of specialization to the domain at the expense of expressive generality.
- Research to identify domains, levels, and commonalities across domains, since languages are needed for each level and domain.
- Research into the architectural level, which cuts across individual domain models. This level deals with the gross function of modules and the ways they are put together (for procedure call, data flow, messages, data sharing, and code mingling). The aggregates defined at this level include "state machine," "object-oriented system," and "pipe/filter system." Contrast this with the programming level, where the issues are algorithms and data structures and the defined entities are procedures and types.
- Research into whether it is possible to implement a concept found in the mechanical engineering environment, the quarter-scale model, and if so, how. A quarter-scale model, which would provide a more precise and detailed correspondence to the desired system than does a conventional prototype, would help to convey the complexity and various design attributes of a software system. It would allow practitioners to better comprehend how well a design works, and it would allow managers to control risk by helping them to understand where problems exist and to better estimate the resources

required to solve those problems. In essence, it would make a seemingly intangible product, software, more real.

- Investigation of the mechanisms for making the transition between and among the various levels of abstraction. This research would involve exploration of automation aspects (e.g., compilers and generators) and computer-aided and manually directed steps. It would also involve exploration of the order of development of the models of a system: Whereas the conventional waterfall life cycle calls for completing each model before translating to the next, other approaches such as rapid prototyping or the spiral model allow for simultaneous development of several models.
- Reformulation of expressions of rigor and technical precision (sometimes referred to as "correctness"), performance given resources, traceability, cost, reliability, and integrity.

Strengthen the Mathematical and Scientific Foundations of Software Engineering

In the absence of a stronger scientific and engineering foundation, complex software systems are often produced by brute force, with managers assigning more and more people to the development effort and taking more and more time. As software engineers begin to envision systems that require many thousands of person-years, current pragmatic or heuristic approaches begin to appear less adequate to meet application needs. In this environment, software engineering leaders are beginning to call for more systematic approaches: More mathematics, science, and engineering are needed (Mills, 1989).

Workshop participants focused on application of such approaches to software analysis; they also affirmed the value of mathematical foundations for better modeling and translation of real-world problems to the abstractions of software systems. Software analysis, which seeks to assure that software works as specified and as designed, is both a significant and a critical part of the implementation of large software systems. Unfortunately, analysis activities have received too little focused attention, and what attention they have received has been largely limited to today's main analytical approach—testing. Testing techniques, moreover, are constantly being discovered and rediscovered.

A more rigorous and comprehensive approach to analysis is needed, one that renders techniques explicit, teaches about them, and develops its own literature and authority. In addition to testing, such techniques as proving, modeling, and simulation should be further developed and targeted to more properties (e.g., safety and functional correctness). Work is needed in performing measurements, establishing metrics, and finding a way to validate them. The understanding of what constitutes a defect and how to verify that designs or code are defect-free is today very limited.

Note that the ability to find defects earlier in the life cycle of a product or to prevent them from being introduced reduces test cost and reduces the number of defects in products delivered to end-users. This ability involves quality assessment and quality assurance. Research questions center on how to specify and measure the attributes (functional, behavioral, and performance) a system must possess in a manner that permits correct generation or proof. What aspects of a product can be assured satisfactorily only by testing as opposed to experimentation? What are the economic trade-offs between developing mathematical proofs and conducting testing? How to design for testability and verifiability is also an issue here.

Promising directions include the application of formal methods (which involve mathematical proofs), exploration of the mechanical and civil engineering concept of a quarter-scale model for previewing a design, application of the "cleanroom concept" (featuring walk-throughs of software with proofs of claims about features rather than checklists of flaws; Mills, 1989), and statistical quality control analogous to that used in manufacturing. A handbook of testing and/or quality assessment is desirable and will be possible with further development of the field of analysis.

NOTES

1. These conclusions are consonant with those of the Defense Science Board Task Force (1987), which focused on management aspects because attitudes, policies, and practices were a major factor in defense software system acquisition.
2. The National Bureau of Standards (now the National Institute of Standards and Technology) drew on several studies to decompose maintenance into corrective maintenance (20 percent), including diagnosis and fixing design, logic, or coding errors; adaptive maintenance (25 percent), which provides for responses to changes in the external environment; perfective maintenance (50 percent or more), which incorporates enhancements; and preventive maintenance (5 percent), which improves future maintainability and reliability (Martin and Osborne, 1983; Swanson and Lientz, 1980). Similarly, experience with U.S. Air Force weapons systems suggests that while 15 to 35 percent of software maintenance corrects design errors, 25 to 50 percent adds new capability, 20 to 40 percent responds to changes in the threat, 10 to 25 percent provides new system interfaces, 10 to 20 percent improves efficiency, 5 to 15 percent improves human factors, and 5 to 10 percent deletes unneeded capability (Mosemann, 1989).
3. An informal query addressed to a community of several hundred software engineering specialists suggested the following candidates: the SAGE missile defense system, the Sabre interactive system for airline reservations, the Yacc compiler tool for UNIX, ARPANET communications software, and the VisiCalc spreadsheet package, among others.
4. To serve this model-definition role, a language must provide five essential capabilities: (1) component suitability—module-level elements, not necessarily compilation units, with function shared by many applications; (2) operators for combining design elements; (3) abstraction—ability to give names to elements for further use; (4) closure—named element can be used like primitives; and (5) specification—more properties than computational functionality, with specifications of composites derivable from specifications of elements.
5. This process of transition is sometimes accomplished manually and sometimes mechanically. Mechanical transitions (e.g., using program generators or compilers) can enhance productivity, but they depend on more precision and understanding than are often available.
6. Overall, the number of levels has grown and shrunk with technology over time. For example, today few people actually code in machine language, and relatively few program in assembly code.

3
Engineering Practice

The phrase "software engineering" was coined in 1968 as an expression of aspiration.[1] It remains today more an aspiration than a description.[2] The field of software engineering lacks the strengths and structure of other engineering disciplines, which have a more highly developed theory and firmer methodological foundations, as well as widely shared tools and techniques. Engineering disciplines are rooted in craftsmanship and evolve through a commercial stage (with emphasis on production and management) before becoming engineering as we generally know it (see Table 3.1). What is needed is a way to define and discuss the "parts" of software engineering, the specifications for each, and a conceptual framework within which to place them. Organizing known techniques and information to identify and describe the parts of the software enterprise and how they fit together would go a long way toward enabling cleaner, more flexible design and development processes (Biggerstaff and Perlis, 1989).

SHORT-TERM ACTIONS

Codify Software Engineering Knowledge for Dissemination and Reuse

Codifying existing software engineering knowledge and disseminating it through handbooks would help achieve several desirable ends: increasing the amount of software that can be created routinely, contributing to knowledge reuse, and ultimately, it is hoped, helping to reduce the size of programs, the time required to develop them, the risk of unacceptable errors, and the tendency to reinvent solutions to the same problems.

For software engineering to progress as a discipline, far more "routine" software development must be produced routinely. At a time when our needs for software are beginning to outstrip our ability to produce it, efforts to reduce the number of tasks requiring human effort are one obvious way to improve the situation. Practice in traditional engineering disciplines includes opportunities for both innovative design (creating things that have not been done before) and routine design (creating yet another example of a class of things that is well understood). Current software practice tends to treat most designs as innovative, even when knowledge exists that should render them routine. There is a need to make the reuse of knowledge routine, something many observers lament is far from happening:

TABLE 3.1 Engineering Evolution

	Craftsmanship	Commercial Practice	Professional Engineering
Practitioners	Virtuosos and amateurs	Skilled craftsmen	Educated professionals
Practice	Intuition and brute force	Established procedure	Analysis and theory
Progress	Haphazard and repetitive	Pragmatic refinement	Scientific
Transmission	Casual and unreliable	Training in mechanics	Education of professionals

SOURCE: "Maybe Your Next Programming Language Shouldn't Be a Programming Language," position statement by Mary Shaw, Appendix B.

> Indeed, if builders built buildings the way many programmers wrote programs, then most of us would still be homeless, because builders, like too many programmers, would be busy reinventing their technology every time they built something new. Continually having to rediscover carpentry, metallurgy, and project management, as well as having to write new building codes, would clearly be enormous disincentives to productivity. . . . (Booch, 1987)

Codifying knowledge and making it more accessible could be an important step in moving toward a situation in which machines can do some of the routine tasks, leaving those more complex and creative tasks to humans.[3] This is one potent way to improve software development productivity. Toward this end, academic researchers can help practitioners by developing a conceptual framework for software elements, routine designs, and standard components, much as chemical engineers have developed a framework for the reuse of design elements at a large scale (Perry et al., 1984).

Reuse of code, a less flexible concept than is reuse of knowledge, is the avenue for minimizing programming effort that has been most widely discussed in the software research and development community (Biggerstaff and Perlis, 1989). Although theoretically attractive, there are many barriers—both technical and sociological—to significantly improving the amount of reuse actually achieved. Achieving reuse involves more than building libraries of programs, and it requires research on what kinds of resuse are feasible, how to index, how to represent reusable elements, and how to deal with variations in the language in which a piece of reusable code is stated or even in the wording of the specification. But so-called code libraries serve as precursors to the broader concept of handbooks discussed below; current work in that area provides a useful starting point.

Develop Software Engineering Handbooks

Software engineering should follow the lead of other engineering fields, which codify basic knowledge and use handbooks as carriers of common knowledge, thereby reducing the tendency for dispersed practitioners to independently develop solutions to common problems, duplicating effort while diluting progress. Handbooks for such disciplines as mechanical and chemical engineering allow a broad sharing of general and specific technical knowledge, which provides a base for further progress. Software engineering needs such products; references during the CSTB workshop to heavily used copies of Don Knuth's multivolume work, *The Art of Computer Programming* (Knuth, 1973), illustrate that a demand exists but remains unmet except in selected, narrow instances.

The structure and contents for software engineering handbooks cannot be determined without progress in accomplishing the codification discussed above. What is clear, however, is that there is a need for substantive as well as process knowledge to be conveyed in these handbooks, and it is that substantive component that distinguishes these handbooks from the manuals that individual organizations use to standardize the software development procedures followed by their employees. Thus handbooks should contain a compendium of algorithms (see, for example, Cody and Waite, 1980), test methods, and items pertaining to design and programming style. Also, to help practitioners work within the practical constraints that they face, handbooks must vary for different domains; the languages, knowledge, and processes associated with, say, transaction processing systems differ from those used for large-scale scientific processing or other types of systems.

Given the dynamic nature of the field, a software engineering handbook should be one that can use computer technology to deliver its contents—an electronic handbook. The goal is to have a repository of information that creates a uniform organization for current knowledge, presents the information accessibly, and provides a means for updating its contents easily.

LONG-TERM ACTIONS

Automate Handbook Knowledge

To maximize the effectiveness of an electronic handbook, advances in several areas that will make such products easy and attractive to use will be necessary. A research initiative aimed at the development of an electronically accessible, interactive software handbook should be inaugurated to develop the following:

- concepts and notations for describing designs and components;
- techniques for organizing and cataloging designs and components;
- techniques and representations for storing, searching, and retrieving designs and components;
- codification of routine designs and components for a large variety of types of software and applications;
- techniques for evaluating designs and components in terms of engineering trade-offs;
- techniques for modeling and simulating systems based on routine designs and components;
- criteria for evaluating and accepting or rejecting handbook entries; and
- technology to make the handbook easily usable and easily accessible.

If the technology and the electronic handbooks can be developed, it will be important to educate software engineers about appropriate methodologies and techniques for using the information they contain. The handbooks themselves will facilitate the teaching of routine design as part of software engineering—itself an important step toward increased productivity. Finally, the handbooks should not only be electronically "recorded," but they should also be built into the standard tools of software engineers, making for a truly activist incarnation.

Nurture Collaboration Among System Developers and Between Developers and Users

Complex software systems are created by the efforts of many people—sometimes as many as a few thousand organized into multiple teams—and frequently no one person has a thorough understanding of the interaction of the entire system. Further, the software developers must communicate with end-users and others to understand the application, the issues, and the requirements. System development is an exercise in collaboration, and it is necessary to maximize the effectiveness of that collaboration. Although the team management problem has captured much attention and concern—much current software engineering consists of ad hoc measures or what could be called "crowd control"—today's measures do not go far enough (MCC, 1986; ACM, 1988; and Bernstein and Yuhas, 1987).

Methodologies for iterative design are necessary. Specifications will always be idealized and simplified, and neither users nor designers are able to envision the full functionality of the resulting system during the traditional design stages. Consequently, system requirements are not so much analytically specified (contrary to appearances) as they are collaboratively evolved through an iterative process of consultation between end-users and software developers. Too many projects or designs have been completed that do not accomplish the desired end because substantive information was not well conveyed or understood in the design or implementation process (Curtis et al., 1988).

Better linkage of knowledge about application areas or domains with software engineering expertise is essential; it is an important direction for exploration. Another involves developing and sustaining a common world view of systems under development. And a third is gaining understanding about how skilled designers make architectural trade-offs in the designs of systems (R. Guindon, 1988; Shaw, 1989).

Better tools to support and enhance cooperative work are necessary in order to provide productivity enhancements; the more time that programmers can spend designing and programming pieces of systems that uniquely require their attention, as opposed to investing their time to overcome communications difficulties, the more likely it is that systems can be built in less time. Various forms of "groupware," tools for computer-supported cooperative work, may prove well suited to the collaborative process of system development. Also, the development of high-speed, ubiquitous computer networks, coupled with sophisticated and easy-to-use resources available through network access, may provide software engineers with valuable research and development tools (CSTB, 1988). For example, the growth of the information services business has illustrated the market potential of data base searching, and handbook implementation will depend critically on network access to data base facilities.

The call for improved collaboration is not new, nor are discussions about computer support for collaboration. But it may be particularly timely, since the motivation in this area is high and new tools are appearing and becoming more economical to use.

NOTES

1. The classic reference is to the software engineering workshop sponsored by the NATO Science Committee in Garmisch, West Germany, October 7-11, 1968.
2. In gross terms, software engineering is concerned with the practical aspects of developing software, such as design under various constraints and economic delivery of software products. It overlaps all of the various specialties of software research, including programming languages, operating systems, algorithms, data structures, data bases, and file systems, and it also addresses such cross-cutting qualities as reliability, security, and efficiency.
3. Thus it could provide a foundation for exploration of user-programmable application generators, which may be appropriate for smaller systems.

4
Research Modes

To complement existing directions in software engineering research and to better address the problem of developing software for large systems, CSTB workshop participants identified a need for cross-fertilization between academic software engineering researchers and practitioners as well as between software engineers and specialists in the behavioral and managerial sciences. CSTB workshop participants also urged universities to encourage additional topics and styles of software engineering research and to seek commensurate funding.

SHORT-TERM ACTION: FOSTER PRACTITIONER AND RESEARCHER INTERACTIONS

There is little academic investigation of the practices, techniques, or problems out in the field today. To rectify this situation, greater interaction among researchers and practitioners is needed as a first step. Such interaction has proved a boon in, for example, manufacturing engineering. Industry and university collaboration in that field has provided researchers and students access to real-world problems and constraints, while providing practitioners with access to creative problem-solving talent and new techniques.

The interaction of academia, industry, and government in software engineering has been inhibited by culture and tradition (Besemer et al., 1986). Although much is known about how complex software systems are built, there are few connections among the various repositories of practical knowledge. Much of the expertise in complex software systems resides in corporations, government research centers, and other nonacademic institutions. It is largely inaccessible to the academic community because of considerations of product delivery, proprietary knowledge, and cultural differences between the corporate and academic communities involved in software research.

That academic computer scientists do not often study large software systems and the process of developing them is one reason that practitioners often feel that the issues studied by academia do not adequately address the problems and challenges faced by builders of large systems—despite an apparently large body of systems analysis, systems design, and other university courses that do address systems issues. This is particularly so, for example, for complex systems involving software embedded in other products or systems (ranging from spacecraft to medical technology) and those systems that involve distributed processes in multiple nonhomogeneous computing and storage elements.

There are a number of reasons that information generated in our universities flows only slowly into the commercial sector: Academics do not study large systems because they do not have them or have access to them, and commercial and academic software specialists tend to read and have their work published in different journals. On the other hand, many topflight corporate researchers and developers, to the extent that they publish at all, do not publish in archival computer science journals because their topics—problems of practice—are not deemed scholarly.

The disparity in perspective and exposure existing between the academic software engineering research community and the practitioners of the corporate world hinders U.S. progress in developing complex software systems. Reducing that disparity is imperative, and it will require a greater degree of interaction between the two groups. Special meetings like the CSTB workshop are but a beginning to this process; implementing an initiative to preserve and study major artifacts, as discussed above, and legitimizing academic exploration of large software systems, discussed below, are other vehicles for interaction.

LONG-TERM ACTIONS

Legitimize Academic Exploration of Large Software Systems

Academic investigation of research topics based on problems encountered in the "real world" by software developers could help industrial and other practitioners in both the short and long terms. For this to happen, new attitudes and incentives must be adopted.

As currently structured, most academic departments are not conducive to large-system research. The tendency of universities to encourage and reward narrow specializations compounds the problem of a lack of opportunity or funding for access to large, complex systems by academic software researchers. Another side of this problem is the focus of the academic world on individual actions, whereas the corporate world is more team oriented. The realities of academic life—funding, tenure tracks, and other career concerns—militate against an individual academic researcher making a strong commitment to large-system research without consideration from the surrounding environment.

Further, whereas industry tends to focus on a problem as it appears in production, researchers (whether corporate or academic) need to find the underlying conceptual problems that are amenable to the development of knowledge that transcends a particular system manifesting a problem. Identification of good research problems based on production problems is a nontrivial problem that itself requires focused efforts. And to pursue that research requires analytical advances, as discussed above, inasmuch as abstract formal models are lacking, language design issues are in eclipse, and testing and measurement have not been formalized.

Funding is a major consideration. Funding of some considerable magnitude is needed if large systems are to be built—which is necessary to determine feasibility—and studied in academic settings, because the artifacts being studied are large. Also, while some universities have state-of-the-art hardware resources (although many do not), universities seldom invest in software tools and tend to lag behind industry in that area. This is a problem because there must be a fit between hardware and software across academic and industrial environments if large artifacts are to be experimented with other than as text (code). Thus it is difficult to study large systems cost effectively. Solving this problem requires innovations in funding, the details of which were beyond the scope of the workshop but which would clearly involve actions by government research funders, universities, and companies (including product development as well as research entities). Another direction for improvement and relief may come from enhanced networking, such as through the proposed national research network, which would allow dispersed researchers to share access to artifacts, other researchers, and practitioners (CSTB, 1988).

If software systems are to be studied in corporate settings, a number of other difficulties will need to be overcome on the industry side. Resolving these difficulties will take much thought and concerted action; the CSTB workshop identified key directions for change. The insights and enhancements that software engineering managers and practitioners seek will come at a price: Industry must be willing to provide support—financial and human resources, and computer resources for experimentation—as well as access to the records of the proprietary system. Mechanisms would be needed to compensate industry for its efforts to produce data in a form useful to researchers or for bearing the risk of experimenting with novel development activities.

Perhaps the biggest concern is protecting the proprietary interests of corporations, for whom large systems are often a source of competitive advantage. Although the academic culture is devoted to openness and information exchange, universities are actively grappling with the problems of protecting corporate proprietary information that are presented by increasing corporate interest in research on practical problems. Business schools appear to have solved this problem some time ago. It should be possible to extend such efforts to apply to academic research into corporate software systems.

Finally, one way to get around some of the difficulties of studying large systems in corporate settings would be to facilitate the study of large systems in government settings. The federal government has been the impetus for the development of large-scale integrated systems, interaction with academic researchers is a long-time tradition for many government organizations, and government entities are more obligated to respond to government programs or mandates. However, inasmuch as federal systems are developed and/or managed by private organizations, limitations on access to design and development processes and personnel may have to be overcome, as in purely corporate settings. Also, some peculiarities of federal systems development are not generalizable to commercial systems. For example, the federal procurement process is associated with specifications that are much more detailed than those typically generated by commercial buyers. Study of federal systems may therefore be an option that is second best.

Glean Insights from Behavioral and Managerial Sciences

There is a need to better understand how groups of people collaborate in large projects involving a variety of participants sharing a rich but uneven distribution of knowledge and imagination among them. Software engineering research would be enhanced by greater interaction with behavioral, managerial, and other scientists that could lead to increasingly effective contributions to software engineering practice, in part by accelerating the transfer of technology into and through the software engineering community. The field has benefited in the past from technology transfer; for example, configuration management practices and change-control techniques developed in the aircraft industry were adopted in the 1950s and 1960s.

There may be particular value in augmenting the insights of computer science and electrical engineering with the insights of behavioral and managerial sciences. Since large software systems will continue to be produced by teams for the foreseeable future, insights gained in other team contexts may be useful for software engineering. To get those insights it may be necessary for software engineers to actually team up with specialists from other disciplines; the benefits of such cross-disciplinary teams have been demonstrated, for example, in the area of ergonomics, where cognitive and management science specialists have been brought in to determine how best to complement human skills with automation. Even within computer science, some areas other than software engineering have aging software platforms that need to be reimplemented to make them less brittle and more easily changed or to improve the user interface to take advantage of workstation technology advances. In such areas software engineers could collaborate with other types of computer scientists and engineers in new developments that both produce new tools and serve as the objects of study. The CSTB workshop pointed to a need for software engineers to glean insight from people with complementary expertise but did not develop the concept.

Develop Additional Directions and Paradigms for Software Engineering Research

Software engineering research today follows a variety of patterns, including the following:

- building systems with certain properties to show their feasibility;
- measuring properties of one or several systems;
- improving the performance of systems along particular dimensions;
- developing abstract formal models for certain domains;
- showing how to describe phenomena by designing languages; and
- making incremental improvements on prior work.

All of these activities are relevant to complex software systems. But given the nature of those systems and the problems we face today, some new approaches to research may also be productive.

Computer Science and Technology Board workshop participants recommended that the academic research community expand its notion of good research to accept review or synthesis studies, case studies, comparative analyses, and development of unifying models for individual or multiple domains. In particular, review or synthesis studies, which are common in a number of other fields, would support a greater and ongoing codification of software engineering knowledge and help to minimize the reinvention of techniques and processes. Finally, if effective handbooks are to be developed, as recommended above, research that supports such handbooks must be encouraged and rewarded.

5
Conclusions

Modern society is increasingly dependent on large, complex computer-based systems and therefore on the software that drives them. In many cases, systems designed 20 years ago still provide a foundation for large businesses—and such systems are becoming unmaintainable. As the ability to manipulate, analyze, and grasp information has been magnified by information systems, so also has the appetite to process more and more information. Each new application has generated ever more complex sets of software systems. In the past few years, problems with such systems have cost millions of dollars, time, and even lives in applications ranging from aviation to controls for medical devices. Improving the quality and the trustworthiness of software systems is a national priority, but it is also a problem that seems forever to receive less attention than it deserves because software systems seem invisible, are poorly understood by laymen, and are not even adequately addressed in universities. Managers are consistently surprised by the inability of software engineers to deliver software on time, within budget, and with expected functionality. The nation should not have to wait for a catastrophe before it tries to enhance this critical resource.

The software research community has ridden the waves of several advances; expert systems and object-oriented programming have been among the topical foci of researchers during this decade. Although large-system developers benefit from these and other advances, the software systems challenge is fundamental and is not amenable to solution through single categories of advances.

As discussed in this report, a necessary first step is for the software engineering community and managers who procure and use large software systems to adopt a more realistic vision of the complex software system development process. Following on, the direction and conduct of software engineering research should be both broadened (in particular, by fostering interactions with practitioners) and made more systematic, through codification and dissemination of knowledge as well as an infusion of more mathematics, science, and engineering. Good problems make good science and engineering—and good problems in the software development community are being bypassed because software engineering researchers are unable to deal with them in a structured, rigorous manner.

The Chinese pictograph for "crisis" is composed of the characters for "danger" and "opportunity." The wisdom this represents is worth noting as we grapple with the looming crisis in our ability to create and maintain large and complex software systems. The danger is that soon we might not be able to create the software our business and government applications need. The opportunity is there for the software engineering research community to find new and fruitful directions in the problems faced by practitioners.

Bibliography

Ad Hoc Committee on the High Cost and Risk of Mission-Critical Software, Report of the USAF Scientific Advisory Board Ad Hoc Committee on the High Cost and Risk of Mission-Critical Software, United States Air Force Scientific Advisory Board, December 1983.

Association for Computing Machinery (ACM) (1988) *Proceedings of Conference on Computer-Supported Cooperative Work*, September 26-28, 1988, Portland, Oregon. New York: ACM.

Balzer, R. (1985) "A 15 Year Perspective on Automatic Programmming." *IEEE Transactions on Software Engineering*, 11(11):1257-1268.

Belady, L. (1989) "Software is the Glue in Large Systems." *IEEE Communications Magazine* (August).

Belady, L., and M. Lehman (1985) *Program Evolution Processes of Software Change*. London: Academic Press Ltd.

Bernstein, L., and C. Yuhas (1987) "The Chain of Command." *UNIX Review* (November).

Besemer, D. J., et al. (1986) "A Synergy of Industrial and Academic Education." Technical Information Series, General Electric Corporate Research and Development, Schenectady, N.Y., (August).

Biggerstaff, T., and A. Perlis (1989) *Software Reusability: Concepts and Models* (Vol. 1) and *Software Reusability: Applications and Experience* (Vol. 2). Addison Wesley/ACM Press Frontiers in Science.

Boehm, B. W. (1981) *Software Engineering Economics*. Englewood Cliffs, N.J.: Prentice-Hall.

Boehm, B. W. (1988) "A spiral model of software development and maintenance." *IEEE Computer 21*, 5 (May 1988), pp. 61-72.

Booch, Grady (1987) *Software Components with Ada*. Menlo Park, Calif.: Benjamin/Cummings Publishing, p. 571.

Bowen, T., G. Wigle, and J. Tsai (1985) *Specification of Software Quality Attributes*. RADC-TR-85-37, Volume 1, Rome Air Development Center.

Brooks, Frederick P., Jr. (1986) "No Silver Bullet—Essence and Accidents of Software Engineering." *Information Processing 86*, H. J. Kugler (ed.), Elsevier Science Publishers B.V. (North-Holland), IFIP.

Cleaveland, J. C. (1988) "Building application generators." *IEEE Software*, (July):25-33.

Cody, William James, Jr. and William McCastline Waite (1980) *Software Manual for the Elementary Functions*. Englewood Cliffs, N.J.: Prentice-Hall, 269 pp.

Computer Science and Technology Board (CSTB), National Research Council (1988) *Toward a National Research Network*. National Academy Press, Washington, D.C.

Curtis, B., H. Krasner, and N. Iscoe (1988) "A Field Study of the Software Design Process." *Communications of the ACM*, 31(11), 1268-1287.

Defense Science Board Task Force on Military Software, *Report of the Defense Science Board Task Force on Military Software*, Office of the Under Secretary of Defense for Acquisition, September 1987.

Freeman, P. (1987) "A conceptual analysis of the draco approach to constructing software systems." *IEEE Transactions on Software Engineering*, (July):830-844.

Guindon, R. (ed.) (1988) *Cognitive Science and Its Applications for Human-Computer Interaction*. Hillsdale, N.J.: Lawrence Erlbaum Associates.

Knuth, Don (1973) *The Art of Computer Programming* (Series title: Addison-Wesley Series in Computer Science and Information Processing. 2 volumes. Second ed.). Reading, Mass.: Addison-Wesley.

Martin, Roger J., and Wilma M. Osborne (1983) "Guidance on Software Maintenance." NBS Special Publication 500-106. Computer Science and Technology, U.S. Department of Commerce, National Bureau of Standards, Washington, D.C., December 1983, p. 6.

McCabe, T. (December 1976) "Complexity Measure." *IEEE Transactions on Software Engineering*, SE-2(4):308-320.

Microelectronics and Computer Technology Corporation (MCC) Conference Committee for CSCW '86 (1986) *Proceedings of Conference on Computer-Supported Cooperative Work*. December 3-5. MCC, Austin, Tex.

Mills, Harlan D. (February 1989) "Benefits of Rigorous Methods of Software Engineering in DoD Software Acquisitions."

Mosemann, Lloyd K. (1989) "Software Engineering and Beyond: The People Problem." Keynote address at the SEI Affiliates Symposium, Software Engineering Institute, Carnegie Mellon University, Pittsburgh, Pa., May 2-4, 1989.

Neighbors, J. M. (1984) "The draco approach to constructing software from reusable components." *IEEE Transactions on Software Engineering*, SE-10(5):564-573.

Partsch, H., and R. Steinbruggen (1983) "Program transformation systems." *ACM Computing Surveys*, 15(3):199-236.

Perry, Robert H., et al. (1984) *Perry's Chemical Engineers' Handbook*. New York: McGraw Hill.

Royce, W. (1970) "Managing the development of large software systems." Proceedings WESCON, August 1970.

Shaw, Mary (1986) "Beyond Programming-in-the-Large: The Next Challenges for Software Engineering." Technical Memorandum SEI-86-TM-6, Software Engineering Institute, Carnegie Mellon University, Pittsburgh, Pa., May 1986.

Shaw, Mary (1989) "Larger Scale Systems Require Higher-Level Abstractions." *Proceedings of the Fifth International Workshop on Software Specification and Design*, May 19-20, 1989, Pittsburgh, Pa. Association for Computing Machinery, New York.

Smith, D., G. Kotik, and S. Westfold (1985) "Research on knowledge-based software environments at Kestrel Institute." *IEEE Transactions on Software Engineering*, 11(11):1278-1295.

Swanson, E. B., and B. Lientz (1980) *Software Maintenance Management: A Study of the Maintenance of Computer Application Software in 487 Data Processing Organizations*. Reading, Mass.: Addison-Wesley.

Williams, B. G., C. K. Mui, B. B. Johnson, and V. Alagappan (1988) "Software Design Issues: A Very Large Information Systems Perspective." Center for Strategic Technology Research, Arthur Andersen & Co., Chicago, September 28, 1988.

Appendixes

Appendixes

Appendix A
Workshop Participants

Victor Vyssotsky, Digital Equipment Corporation (Workshop *Chair*)
Frances E. Allen,* IBM T. J. Watson Research Center
David R. Barstow,* Schlumberger Wells Gerris
Laszlo A. Belady,* Microelectronics and Computer Technology Corporation (MCC)
Larry Bernstein,* AT&T Bell Laboratories
Richard B. Butler,* IBM Corporation
Thomas A. Corbi,* IBM Corporation
John D. Gannon, National Science Foundation
Susan L. Gerhart,* Microelectronics and Computer Technology Corporation (MCC)
Barry M. Horowitz,* The MITRE Corporation
Bruce B. Johnson,* Arthur Andersen and Company
Anita Jones,* University of Virginia
Kenneth Kochbeck, McDonnell Douglas Corporation
Harlan D. Mills,* Information Systems
John B. Munson,* Unisys Corporation
Douglas T. Ross,* SofTech, Inc.
Winston Royce,* SoftwareFirst
Mary Shaw,* Carnegie Mellon University
Charles Simonyi,* Microsoft Corporation
Shmuel Winograd, IBM T. J. Watson Research Center
Stephen Wolfram, University of Illinois at Urbana-Champaign
William A. Wulf,* National Science Foundation
Andres G. Zellweger,* CTA, Inc.
Arthur I. Zygielbaum,* Jet Propulsion Laboratory

Staff

Marjory S. Blumenthal, CSTB
C. Kristina Gunsalus, CSTB Consultant
Pamela R. Rodgers, CSTB Consultant
Donna F. Allen, Administrative Secretary

---

*Position statement appears in Appendix B.

Appendix B
Position Statements

Prior to the workshop, participants were asked to submit position statements that responded to the following two questions:

1. What do you consider to be the worst problem you have with current software production, and what suggestions do you have for alleviating it?
2. What do you see as the most critical problem that industry and the nation have with current software production, and what solutions do you suggest?

Some participants revised their statements as a result of workshop deliberations. These statements are presented as submitted by the authors, with some standardization of format.

FRANCES E. ALLEN

The worst problem I have with current software production is transferring prototyped ideas developed in a computer science environment to product software useful to customers. Technology transfer between different groups is frequently difficult but transferring technologies and requirements between two very different cultures is doubly difficult. Users of software have reliability and economic (speed, space, cost) constraints that are of little interest to the computer scientist; the computer scientist has solutions which, when properly engineered, could greatly enhance products.

I believe there are three ways of alleviating the problem. One way is to develop a technology for measuring and evaluating the effectiveness of an approach when applied to a given problem. We have ways of evaluating the complexity and correctness of an algorithm; we need ways of evaluating and predicting the appropriateness of specific software solutions to specific problems. In other words, software engineering must become a science with accepted and validated predictive metrics.

The second way of alleviating the problems of moving ideas and prototypes to market is to build usable prototypes. (I will discuss this below.)

The third way of alleviating the problem is education. Computer scientists must become more relevant and must understand the realities of the market place.

The most critical problem that industry and the nation have with current software production is the number of lines of code needed to accomplish a function. Many production and maintenance costs can be correlated to the number of KLOCs (thousands of lines of code) needed. Programmers produce X KLOCs a year and Y errors occur per Z KLOC. But each KLOC isn't providing much function. If programs were written in much higher level languages then many fewer KLOCs would be required to do the same job. So though the X, Y, Z numbers might stay the same, fewer programmers would be needed and fewer errors would occur.

Moving to very high level languages requires compiler technology which effectively maps the program to the underlying system without loss of efficiency. Much of that technology exists today. I recommend a concentrated effort on expanding that technology and exploiting it in the context of very high level languages.

This proposal runs counter to what is happening today with C emerging as a major systems language. C is regressive in that it was designed to allow and generally requires that the user optimize his program. Hence, users of the language are spending time and effort doing what compilers can do as well or better in many cases. What has been gained? More KLOCs but not more productivity, more function or fewer errors.

DAVID R. BARSTOW

Currently, Schlumberger's most significant software problem is duplication of effort: we often write several times what appears to be essentially the same software. One solution to the problem is to maintain an extensive software library, but this approach is complicated by a diversity of target machines and environments. A second solution would be to develop sophisticated programming environments that present to the user a higher level computational model, coupled with translators that automatically produce code for different targets.

The most critical software problem faced by industry and the nation is the cost of maintenance and evolution: most studies of software costs indicate that over two-thirds of the cost of a large system is incurred after the system is delivered. These costs cannot be reduced completely, of course, since uses and expectations about a software system will naturally change during the system's lifetime. But much of the cost is due to the fact that a considerable amount of information, such as the rationale for design and implementation decisions, is lost during development and must be reconstructed by the maintainers and evolvers of the system. One way to address this problem would be to develop knowledge-based techniques for explicitly representing such information so that it could be stored during development and referenced during evolution. One good way to develop such techniques would be through case studies of existing large systems, perhaps through collaborative efforts between industry and academia.

LASZLO A. BELADY

Worst Problem—Possible Solution

Since large scale software development is a labor intensive activity, look for the problem where people spend the most time. Through our field studies of industry MCC found that the predominant activity in complex system development is the participants' teaching and instructing each other. Users must teach the software engineers about the application domain, and vice versa; designers of subsystems must describe the intricacies of their work to other designers, and later to implementors; and since the process is rather iterative, this mutual teaching happens several times and in several participant groupings. Indeed, most of the time *all* project participants must be ready to transmit the knowledge they have acquired about the emerging product and to analyze together the consequences on the total systems of local (design) decisions.

Even more importantly, experience gathered in the computer aided system project setting could spawn much needed efforts in computer aiding the training and re-training process needed everywhere to keep the nation's workforce attuned to changing circumstances, and thus competitive.

Perhaps the experience accumulated over decades in Computer Aided Instruction (CAI) must be tuned, applied and refined for the complex system development process. Results from AI could also be applied to help eliminate the "teaching" overload for all involved.

Industry/National Problem

Software is the glue that holds the islands of computer applications in distributed systems. For the next decades this gradual integration into networks will take place in each industry, between enterprises, at the national level and beyond. The resulting systems will be built out of off-the-shelf software and hardware components, where each integrated subsystem is unique and must be designed individually by a team of experts: users, managers, application specialists, programmers.

The design of these "hetero-systems" needs fundamentally new approaches, in particular:

- efficient, cooperative, project teamwork augmented by computer technology (which will be applicable everywhere where people must work tightly together, not only in the computer industry)
- convergence of hardware-software design; in fact, a deliberate shift in basic education is also needed to create interdisciplinary "system designers" instead of separate hardware and software professionals.

But, more importantly, experience gathered in the computer aided system project setting could spawn much needed efforts in computer aiding the training and re-training process.

LARRY BERNSTEIN

Worst Problem Facing Me in Software Productivity

Software architecture problems are the most difficult for me. The solution requires problem solving skills with a heavy dose of the ability to do engineering trade-offs. People trained in computer science do not often bring these skills to the work place. We cannot teach them in two- to four-week short courses, so we often suffer while rookies learn on the job. Studies of computer science curricula in the ACM pointed out the lack of problem-solving skills in the typical computer science curriculum (*Computing as a Discipline*, Peter J. Denning, Douglas E. Commer, David Gries, Michael C. Mulder, Allen Tucker, A. Joe Turner, and Paul R. Young, Report of the ACM Task Force on the Core of Computer Science, January 1989, Vol. 32, No. 1). Those with a bachelor's degree are often mechanics who know how to program, but do not know how to decide what problem needs solving, or what alternatives there are for its solution.

Making four semesters of engineering science a requirement for computer scientists is a minimal solution. Apprenticeships and identifying software architectures are quite useful. Prototypes are helpful to make design decisions quantitative rather than qualitative.

Worst Problems Facing the Country in Software Productivity

Too often funders, customers, and managers are willing to be "low balled" on effort estimation. The lack of appreciation for up front capitalization in the software industry with consequential failures points to a serious problem confronting us. It leads to the scattered and slow application of proven techniques to enhance productivity and fosters a climate for hucksters to sell their latest all purpose course to those ailing projects.

A technology platform incorporating proven approaches would facilitate technology transfer from universities to industry and between companies. Changes are needed to permit and foster such cooperation between competitors. Ties of U.S. companies to Japanese companies will speed the growth of the Japanese as viable software competitors, yet we discourage similar ties in the United States. We need to have joint research with Japan and Canada so as to foster a market where each benefits and contributes to the extension of software technology. Various *Harvard Business Review* articles have dealt with capitalization and the introduction of technology.

Recommendation

A specific research recommendation is to regularize design by creating a handbook which would:

- organize software knowledge,
- provide canonical architectures,
- provide algorithms in a more usable way than Knuth did,
- facilitate understanding of constraints, domains of application, and tradeoff analysis, and
- foster codification of routine designs that can then be taught and used by journeyman architects.

A second issue is to focus on software (not just code!) reuse. Specific items to tackle include:

- Determine when structured interfaces between subsystems with different models of the problem domain are sufficient and when integration by designing to a single model of the problem domain is necessary.
  - Develop benefit models for justifying investment in making software reusable.
  - Classify architecture which will encourage reuse.
  - Determine how much reuse is possible with current prices.

- Develop indexing and cataloging techniques to find reusable elements.

A new theory of testing is needed to design software that is testable to certify quality.

On Design for Testability

How do you specify the attributes (functional and non-functional) a system must possess in a manner which permits correct generation or proof?
What attributes are only verifiable by testing?
What are the economic trade-offs between proofs and testing?

On Certifying Quality

Classify quality certification methods and measures effective in real (large) projects for functional and non-functional performance. Examples include the following:

- Proof of correctness.
- Theory of stochastic software usage.
- Functional scenario testing is thirty times more effective than coverage testing.

We need to build systems in anticipation of change by understanding the correct granularity of components and forcing localization of change.

RICHARD B. BUTLER AND THOMAS A. CORBI

Program Understanding: Challenge for the 1990's

Abstract

There are a variety of motivators[1] which are continuing to encourage corporations to invest in software tools and training to increase software productivity, including: increased demand for software; limited supply of software engineers; rising software engineer support expectations (e.g., for CASE tools); and reduced hardware costs. A key motivator for software tools and programmer education in the 1990's will be software evolved over decades from several thousand line, sequential programming systems into multi-million line, multi-tasking *complex* systems.

This paper discusses the nature of maturing complex systems. Next, it examines current software technology and engineering approaches to address continuing development of these systems. Program understanding is identified as a key element which supports many development activities. Lack of training and education in understanding programs is identified as an inhibitor. Directions to encourage development of new software tools and engineering techniques to assist the process of understanding our industry's *existing complex systems* are suggested.

Maturing Complex Systems

As the programming systems written in the 1960's and 1970's continue to mature, the focus for software tools and programmer education will shift from tools and techniques to help develop new programming projects to analysis tools and training to help us understand and enhance maturing complex programming systems.

In the 1970's, the work of Belady and Lehman[2-4] strongly suggested that *all* large programs will undergo significant change during the in-service phase of their lifecycle, regardless of the *a priori* intentions of the organization. Clearly, they were right. As an industry, we have continued to grow and change our large software systems to

- remove defects,
- address new requirements,
- improve design and/or performance,
- interface to new programs,
- adjust to changes in data structures or formats,
- exploit new hardware and software features, and
- scale up the new architectures and processing power.

As we extended the lifetimes of our systems by continuing to modify and enhance them, we also increased our already significant data processing investments in them and continued to increase our reliance on them. Complex software systems have grown to be significant assets in many companies.

However, as we introduce changes and enhancements into our maturing systems, the structure of the systems begins to deteriorate. Modifications alter originally "clean" designs. Fix is made upon fix. Data structures are altered. Members of the "original" programming teams disperse. Once "current" documentation gradually becomes outdated. System erosion takes its toll and key systems steadily become less and less maintainable and increasingly difficult, error prone, and expensive to modify.

Flaherty's[5] study indicates the effect on productivity of modifying product code compared to producing new code. His data for the studied S/370 communications, control, and language software show that productivity differences were greater between the ratio of changed source code to total amount of code than productivity differences between the different kinds of product classes—productivity was lowest when changing less than 20% of the total code in each of the products studied. The kind of software seemed to be a less important factor related to lower productivity than did the attribute of changing a small percentage of the total source code of the product. Does this predict *ever decreasing programmer productivity for our industry* as we change small percentages of maturing complex systems?

Clearly as systems grow older, larger, and more complex, the challenges which will face tomorrow's programming community will be even more difficult than today's. Even the *Wall Street Journal* stereotypes today's "beeper carrying" programmer who answers the call when catastrophe strikes:

> He is so vital because the computer software he maintains keeps blowing up, threatening to keep paychecks from being issued or invoices from being mailed. He must repeatedly ride to the rescue night and day because the software, altered repeatedly over the years, has become brittle. Programming problems have simply gotten out of hand.
>
> Corporate computer programmers, in fact, now spend 80% of their time just repairing the software and updating it to keep it running. Developing new applications in this patchwork quilt has become so muddled that many companies can't figure out where all the money is going.[6]

The skills needed to do today's programming job have become much more diverse. To successfully modify some aging programs, programmers have become part historian, part detective, and part clairvoyant. Why?

"Software renewal" or "enhancement" programming is quite different from the kind of idealized software engineering programming taught in university courses:

> The major difference between new development and enhancement work is the enormous impact that the base system has on key activities. For example, while a new system might start with exploring users' requirements and then move into design, an enhancements project will often force the users' requirements to fit into existing data and structural constraints, and much of the design effort will be devoted to exploring the current programs to find out how and where new features can be added and what their impact will be on existing functions.
>
> The task of making functional enhancements to existing systems can be likened to the architectural work of adding a new room to an existing building. The design will be severely constrained by the existing structure, and both the architect and the builders must take care not to weaken the existing structure when the additions are made. Although the costs of the new room usually will be lower than the costs of constructing an entirely new building, the costs per square foot may be much higher because of the need to remove existing walls, reroute plumbing and electrical circuits and take special care to avoid disrupting the current site.[7]

The industry is becoming increasingly mired in these kinds of application software "renovation" and maintenance problems. Parikh[8] reports the magnitude of the problem:

- Results of a survey of 149 managers of MVS installations with programming staffs ranging from 25-800 programmers indicating that maintenance tasks (program fixes/modifications) represent from 55 to 95% of their work load.
- Estimates that $30B is spent each year on maintenance ($10B in the US) with 50% of most companies' DP budgets going to maintenance and that 50-80% of the time of an estimated 1M programmers or programming managers is spent on maintenance.
- An MIT study which indicates that for every $1 allocated for a new development project, $9 will be spent on maintenance for the life cycle of the project.

Whereas improved design techniques, application generators, and wider usage of reusable software parts may help alleviate some aspects of the "old code" problem,[9] until these approaches take widespread hold in our critical complex systems, programmers will need tools and training to assist in reconstructing and analyzing information in previously developed and modified systems. Even when more "modern" software development techniques and technologies are widespread, new and unanticipated requirements for "ities" (e.g., usability, installability, reliability, integrity, security, recoverability, reconfigurability, serviceability, etc.) which are not yet taught in software engineering, are not yet part of the methodology being used, and are not yet "parameters" to the code generator will necessitate rediscovery and rework of our complex systems.

Approaches to Maturing Complex Systems

The notion of providing tools for program understanding is not new. Work in the 1970's[10-14] which grew out of the program proving, automatic programming and debugging, and artificial intelligence efforts first broached the subject. Researchers stressed how rich program descriptions (assertions, invariants, etc.) could automate error detection and debugging. The difficulty in modelling interesting problem domains and representing programming knowledge, coupled with the problems of symbolic execution, has inhibited progress. While there has been some limited success,[15] the lack of fully implemented, robust systems capable of "understanding" and/or debugging a wide range of programs underscores the difficulty of the problem and the shortcomings of these AI-based approaches.

Recognizing the growing "old program" problem in the applications area, entrepreneurs have transformed this problem into a business opportunity and are marketing "code restructuring" tools. A variety of restructuring tools have emerged (see reference 16 for an examination of restructuring). The restructuring approach to address "old" programs has had mixed success. While helpful in some cases to clean up some modules, in other cases restructuring does not appear to help.

One government study[17] has shown positive effects which can result from restructuring include some reduced maintenance and testing time, more consistency of style, reduced violations of local coding and structure standards, better learning, and additional structural documentation output from restructuring tools. However, on the negative side: the initial source may not be able to be successfully processed by some restructurers requiring modification before restructuring; compile times, load module size, and execution time for the restructured program can increase; human intervention may be required to provide meaningful names for structures introduced by the tool.

Movement and replacement of block commentary is problematic for some restructurers. And, as has been observed, overall system control and data structures which have eroded over time are not addressed:

> If you pass an unstructured, unmodular mess through one of these restructuring systems, you end up with at best, a structured, unmodular mess. I personally feel modularity is more important than structured code; I have an easier time dealing with programs with a bunch of GOTO's than one with it's control logic spread out over the entire program.[18]

In general, automatically re-capturing a design from source code, at the present state of the art, is not considered feasible. But some work is underway and some success has been reported. Sneed et al.[19,20] have been working with a unique set of COBOL tools which can be used to assist in rediscovering information about old code via static analysis, to interactively assist in re-modularizing and then restructuring, and finally to generate new source code representation of the original software. Also, research carried out jointly by CRIAI (Consorzio Campano di Ricerca per l'Informatica e l'Automazione Industriale) and DIS (Dipartimento di Informatica e Sistemistica at the University of Naples) reports[21] the automatic generation of low level Jackson or Warnier/Orr documents which are totally consistent with COBOL source code.

Both Sneed and CRIAI/DIS agree, however, that determining higher level design abstractions will require additional knowledge outside that which can be analyzed directly from the source code.

The experience of IBM's Federal Systems Division with the aging Federal Aviation Administration's National Airspace System (NAS)[22] seems to indicate that the best way out is to relearn the old software relying primarily on the source code, to rediscover the module and data structure design, and to use a structured approach[23-25] of formally recording the design in a design language which supports the data typing, abstract types, control structures, and data abstraction models.

This often proved to be an iterative process (from very detailed design levels to more abstract), but it resulted in a uniform means of understanding and communicating about the original design. The function and state machine models then provided the designer a specification from which, subsequently, to make changes to the source code.

The need to expand "traditional" software engineering techniques to encompass reverse engineering design and to address "software redevelopment" has been recognized elsewhere:

> The principal technical activity of software engineering is moving toward something akin to "software redevelopment." Software redevelopment means taking an existing software description (e.g., as expressed in a programming or very high level language) and transforming it into an efficient, easier-to-maintain realization portable across local computing environments. This redevelopment technology would ideally be applicable to both 1) rapidly assembled system prototypes into production quality systems, and 2) old procrustean software developed 3 to 20 years ago still in use and embedded in ongoing organization routines but increasingly difficult to maintain.[26]

Understanding Programs: a Key Activity

With our aging software systems, studies indicate that *"more than half of the programmer's task is understanding the system."*[27] The Fjeldstat-Hamlen study[28] found that, in making an enhancement, maintenance programmers *studied the original program*

- about three-and-a-half times as long as they studied the documentation, and
- just as long as they spent implementing the enhancement.

In order to work with "old" code, today's programmers are forced to spend most of their time studying the only really accurate representation of the system.

To understand a program, there are three things you can do: read about it (e.g., documentation); read it (e.g., source code); or run it (e.g., watch execution, get trace data, examine dynamic storage, etc.). Static analysis (control flow, data flow, cross reference) can augment reading the source. Documentation can be excellent or it can be misleading. Studying the dynamic behavior of an executing program can be very useful and can dramatically improve understanding by revealing program characteristics which cannot be assimilated from reading the source code alone. But the source code is usually the primary source of information.

While we all recognize that "understanding" a program is important, most often it goes unmentioned as an explicit task in most programmer job or task descriptions. Why? The process of understanding a piece of code is not an explicit deliverable in a programming project. Sometimes a junior programmer will have an assignment to "learn this piece of code"—oddly, as if it were a one time activity.

Experienced programmers who do enhancement programming realize, just as architects and builders doing a major renovation, that they must repeatedly examine the actual existing structure. Old architectural designs and blueprints may be of some use, but to be certain that a modification will be successful, they must discover or rediscover and assemble detailed pieces of information by going to the "site." In programming, regardless of the "waterfall" or "iterative" process, this kind of investigation happens at various points along the way:

- While requirements are being examined, lead designers or developers are typically navigating through the existing code base to get a rough idea of the size of the job, the areas of the system which will be impacted, and the knowledge and skills which will be needed by the programming team which does the work.
- As design proceeds from the high level to low level, each of the team members repeatedly examines the existing code base to discover how the new function can be grafted onto the existing data structures and into the general control flow and data flow of the existing system.
- Wise designers may tour the existing code to get an idea of performance implications which the enhancement may have on various critical paths through the existing system.
- Just before the coding begins, programmers are looking over the "neighborhood" of modules which will be involved in the enhancement. They are doing the planning of the detailed packaging—separating the low level design into pieces which must be implemented by new

modules or which can be fit into existing modules. Often, they are building the lists of new and changed modules and macros for the configuration management or library control team who need this information in order to re-integrate the new and changed source code when putting the pieces of the system back together again.

- During the coding phase, programmers are immersed in the "old code". Programmers are constantly making very detailed decisions to re-write or restructure existing code vs. decisions to change the existing code by deleting, moving, and adding a few lines here and a few lines there. Understanding the existing programs is also key to adding new modules: how to interface to existing functions in the old code? how to use the existing data structures properly? how not to cause unwanted side effects?

- A new requirement or two and a few design changes usually come into focus after the programmers have left the starting blocks. "New code" has just become "old code". Unanticipated changes must be evaluated as to their potential impact to the system and whether or not these proposed changes can be contained in the current schedules and resources. The "old base" and the "new evolving" code under development must be scrutinized to supplement the intuitions of the lead programmers before notifying management of the risks.

- Testers may delve into the code if they are using "white box" techniques. Sometimes even a technical writer will venture into the source code to clarify something for a publication under revision.

- Debugging, dump reading, and trace analysis constantly require long terminal sessions of "program understanding" where symptoms are used to postulate causes. Each hypothesis causes the programmer to go exploring the existing system to find the source of the bug. And when the problem is found, then a more "bounded" exploration is usually required to gather the key information required to actually build the fix and insert yet another modification into the system.

Therefore, the program understanding process is a crucial sub-element in achieving many of the project deliverables: sizings, high level design, low level design, build plan, actual code, debugged code, fixes, etc.

The programmer attempts to understand a programming systems so he can make informed decisions about the changes he is making. The literature refers to this "understanding process" as "program comprehension":

> The program comprehension task is a critical one because it is a subtask of debugging, modification, and learning. The programmer is given a program and is asked to study it. We conjecture that the programmer, with the aid of his or her syntactic knowledge of the language, constructs a multileveled internal semantic structure to represent the program. At the highest level the programmer should develop an understanding of what the program does: for example, this program sorts an input tape containing fixed-length records, prints a word frequency dictionary, or parses an arithmetic expression. This high-level comprehension may be accomplished even if low-level details are not fully understood. At low semantic levels the programmer may recognize familiar sequences of statements or algorithms. Similarly, the programmer may comprehend low-level details without recognizing the overall pattern of operation. The central contention is that programmers develop an internal semantic structure to represent the syntax of the program, but they do not memorize or comprehend the program in a line-by-line form based on syntax.[29]

Learning to Understand Programs

While software engineering (e.g., applied computer science) appears as a course offering in many university and college Computer Science departments, "software renewal", "program comprehension", or "enhancement programming" is absent. When you think in terms of the skills which are needed as our software assets grow and age, lack of academic training in "how to go about understanding programs" will be a major inhibitor to programmer productivity in the 1990's.

> ... Unfortunately, a review by the author of more than 50 books on programming methodologies revealed almost no citations dealing with the productivity of functional enhancements, except a few minor observations in the context of maintenance.

> The work of functional enhancements to existing software systems is underreported in the software

engineering curriculums, too, and very few courses exist in which this kind of programming is even discussed, much less taught effectively.[7]

For other "language" disciplines, classical training includes learning to speak, read, and write. Reading comprehension is partner with composition and rhetoric. In school, we are required to read and critique various authors. An English education curriculum does not teach "basic language skills" (programming language syntax and semantics), "recommended sentence structures" (structural programming), and "short stories" (algorithms), expecting students to be fully trained, productive copy editors/authors for major publications. Yet, many Computer Science departments sincerely believe that they are preparing their students to be ready for the workplace.

Unfortunately, most new college graduates entering today's software industry must confront a very considerable "learning curve" about an existing system before they get to the point where they can begin to try to do design or coding. They have little or no training nor much tool assistance to do this. Acquiring programming comprehension skills has been left largely to "on-the-job" training while trying to learn about an existing system.[30] Even experienced programmers can have trouble moving to a different project.

The lack of training and tools to help in understanding large, "old" programming systems also has another negative effect on productivity. It is resulting in a kind of job stagnation throughout the industry which Boehm terms the "Inverse Peter Principle".[31]

> The Inverse Peter Principle: "People rise to an organizational position in which they become irreplaceable, and get stuck there forever." This is most often encountered in software maintenance, where a programmer becomes so uniquely expert on the inner complexities and operating rituals of a piece of software that the organization refuses to let the person work on anything else. The usual outcome is for the programmer to leave the organization entirely, leaving an even worse situation.

As a large programming system grows older and older, more and more talented programmers will "get stuck" due to the "Inverse Peter Principle". "Getting stuck" directly impacts attempts by management to maximize project productivity by assigning the most talented programmers to get the next job done. Therefore, a lack of program understanding, training, and tools is a productivity inhibitor for new programmers on a project as well as a career inhibitor for the key project "gurus". As our programming systems grow in age, size, and complexity, these problems will compound, becoming increasingly more acute.

Directions

An industry focus on "Software Renewal" tools and programmer education is needed to reduce the costs to modify and maintain large complex programming systems, to improve our understanding of our programs so we can continue to extend their life and restructure them as needed, and to build bridges from old software to new design techniques and notations and reuse technologies.

Just as library and configuration control systems were developed when the volumes of source code and the numbers of programmers working on a system increased, it is inevitable that new tools systems for managing the information about large programming systems will emerge to support long term "software renewal".

Just as software engineering education evolved to guide development of new programming systems, new concepts and techniques must be developed to assist programmers in re-discovering the properties and understanding our long-lived, complex systems.

Software engineering has an opportunity to develop new methods for implanting "guideposts" so that the next generation's programmer can more easily gain insight into the rationale of past programming.

References

1. Barry W. Boehm, Maria H. Penedo, E. Don Stuckle, Robert D. Williams, and Arthur B. Pyster, "A Software Development Environment for Improving Productivity," IEEE Computer, 17, No. 6, 30-44, June (1984).
2. L.A. Belady and M.M. Lehman, "A Model of Large Program Development," IBM Systems Journal, 15, No. 3, 225-252, (1976).
3. M.M. Lehman and F.H. Parr, "Program Evolution and its Impact on Software Engineering," Proceedings of the 2nd International Conference on Software Engineering, San Francisco, October (1976).
4. M. M. Lehman, "Laws of Evolution Dynamics - Rules and Tools for Programming Management," Proceedings of the Infotech Conference on Why Software Projects Fail, London, April (1978).
5. M.J. Flaherty, "Programming process measurement for the System/370," IBM Systems Journal, 24, No. 2, 172-173, (1985).
6. Paul B. Carroll, "Computer Glitch: Patching Up Software Occupies Programmers And Disables Systems," Wall Street Journal, 1, January 22, (1988).
7. Capers Jones, "How not to measure programming quality," Computerworld, 82, January 20 (1986).
8. Girish Parikh, "Making the Immortal Language Work," International Computer Programs Business Software Review, 33, April (1987).
9. Ronald A. Radice and Richard W. Phillips, Software Engineering: An Industrial Approach, Volume 1, pp. 14-19, Prentice Hall, Englewood Cliffs, 1988.
10. I.P. Goldstein, "Summary of MYCROFT: A system for understanding simple picture programs," Artifical Intelligence, 6, 249-277, (1975).
11. S.M. Katz and Z. Manna, "Toward automatic debugging of programs," SIGPLAN Notices, 10, 143-155, (1975).
12. G.R. Ruth, "Intelligent program analysis," Artifical Intelligence, 7, 65-87, (1976).
13. S.M. Katz and Z. Manna, "Logical analysis of programs," Communications of the ACM, 19, 188-206, (1976).
14. F.J. Lukey, "Understanding and debugging programs," International Journal of Man-Machine Studies, 12, 189-202, (1980).
15. W.L. Johnson and E. Soloway, "PROUST: Knowledge Based Program Understanding," Proceedings of the Seventh International Conference on Software Engineering, Orlando, FL, March (1984).
16. Robert S. Arnold, editor. Tutorial on Software Restructuring, IEEE Computer Society Press, Washington, DC, 1986.
17. Parallel Test and Evaluation of a Cobol Restructuring Tool, U.S. General Accounting Office, September 1987.
18. Irv Wendel, "Software tools of the Pleistocene," Software Maintenance News, 4, No. 10, 20, October (1986).
19. H.M. Sneed, "Software Renewal: A Case Study," IEEE Software, 1, No. 3, 56-63, July (1984).
20. H.M. Sneed and G. Jandrasics, "Software Recycling," IEEE Conference on Software Maintenance, 82-90, Austin, TX, September (1987).
21. P. Antonini, P. Benedusi, G. Cantone, and A. Cimitile, "Maintenance and Reverse Engineering: Low-Level Design Documents Production and Improvement," IEEE Conference on Software Maintenance, 91-100, Austin, TX, September (1987).
22. Robert N. Britcher and James J. Craig, "Using Modern Design Practices to Upgrade Aging Software Systems," IEEE Software, 3, No. 3, 16-24, May (1986).
23. A.D. Ferrentino and H.D. Mills, " State Machines and their Semantics in Software Engineering," Proceedings of COMPSAC '77, 242-251, (1977).

24. R.C. Linger, H.D. Mills, and B.I. Witt, Structured Programming Theory and Practice, Addison-Wesley, Reading, MA, 1979.
25. H.D. Mills, D. O'Neill, R.C. Linger, M. Dyer, and R.E. Quinnan, "The management of software engineering," IBM Systems Journal, 19, No. 4, 414-477, (1980).
26. Walt Scacchi, "Managing software engineering projects: A social analysis," IEEE Transactions on Software Engineering, SE-10, No. 1, 49-59, January (1984).
27. Girish Parikh and Nicholas Zvegintzov, editor. Tutorial on Software Maintenance, p. ix, IEEE Computer Society Press, Silver Spring, MD, 1983.
28. R.K. Fjeldstad and W.T. Hamlen, "Application Program Maintenance Study: Report to Our Respondents," Proceedings of GUIDE 48, The Guide Corporation, Philadelphia, PA, (1979).
29. B. Shneiderman and R. Mayer, "Syntactic/Semantic Interactions in Programmer Behavior: A Model and Experimental Results," International Journal of Computer and Information Science, 8, No. 3, 219-238, (1979).
30. Carolynn Van Dyke, "Taking 'Computer Literacy' Literally," Communications of the ACM, 30, No. 5, 366-374, May (1987).
31. Barry W. Boehm, Software Engineering Economics, p. 671, Prentice-Hall, Inc., Englewood Cliffs, NJ, 1981.

RICHARD B. BUTLER AND THOMAS A. CORBI

Japan: Nationally Coordinated R&D for the Information Industry

Abstract

A healthy, growing, competitive U.S. software industry is a key element to the national security and to well-being of the American economy. Not only is software an important industry in itself, but complex system's software is key to providing leadership in computer hardware. It is also the technological enabler to the full spectrum of energy, retail, manufacturing, transportation, construction, and financial industries and to education, government, and the military. Today's complex software systems will continue to evolve to provide the supporting information services needed and brand new complex systems will emerge.

Ever improving U.S. software technology research and development and growing computer literacy are crucial to our industry and nation, if we are to continue to compete worldwide in developing new complex software systems to support future economic growth. The alternatives are either to fall behind the world-wide competition in the spectrum of industries dependent on complex systems technology or to become increasingly dependent on foreign nations as suppliers of this technology.

This paper briefly examines Japan's coordinated research and development of various software technologies and computer literacy efforts. The pattern has been widely discussed in the literature. MITI jointly develops goals with industry and for education. Western technology is closely studied. Western developments are reduced to practice. Incremental improvements are made. Competitive product offerings emerge and are then exported.

Development of a U.S. national agenda to coordinate and accelerate research and development of software technologies and to improve computer literacy is suggested.

MITI Goal Setting

> NEW HAVEN, Conn.—IBM's toughest competition is not coming from U.S. companies, but from the Japanese, IBM's chairman and chief executive officer, John F. Akers, said Monday.
>
> The Japanese have created full product lines, technological capabilities, flexible alliances and worldwide distribution networks, Akers said, in citing their accomplishments to students at Yale University's School of Organization and Management.
>
> Akers listed a number of companies in Europe and the United States, but he said: "The Japanese are the toughest. No question about it."[1]

Since 1970, the Japanese government has been promoting research and development activities in the "Information Industry" through its Ministry of International Trade and Industry (MITI). MITI has identified the "Information Industry" as a probable successor to steel and automobiles, has been steering legislation through the Japanese Diet (like our Congress), has set long-term national directions and goals, has established phased projects to work toward those goals, and has funded forward-looking research and promoted cooperative ventures among the Japanese Computer Manufacturers (JCMs).

In 1970, the Diet passed a law submitted by MITI to promote Information Technology with a central body to coordinate various actions and plans. This organization was called the Information Technology Promotion Agency (IPA). The program has received significant funding. For example, MITI's government support and loans from the Japan Development Bank for IPA committed about $373 Million for hardware (includes 5th generation project) and $566 Million for software through fiscal year 1986. Reportedly, the participating JCMs invest 2 to 3 dollars for every dollar invested by MITI.

MITI's direction and influence are widely reported in the computer trade press. MITI's visions for the Information Industry have been released every 5 to 7 years for the purpose of gaining private sector consensus in order to develop national industrial policy. Significant reports have been issued in 1976, 1981, and 1987. In developing the June 1987 report, IBM Japan and AT&T International (Japan), Ltd. representatives were included for the first time as part of a group of 30 individuals formed by the Basic Policy Committee of the MITI's Information Industry Structure Council. The 1987 MITI report, titled "A Vision of the Information Industry in the Year 2000" has been commented on by the Japanese press.[2]

The report clearly states, "It is expected that the information industry will eventually become a mainstay to replace the steel and automobile industries." This kind of a change implies a significant shift in the Japanese economy. It spells out Japan's objectives underscoring their serious, long term commitment to such topics as:

- Continued needs for faster, more sophisticated hardware with new function.
- Continued push on lower costs and better price-performance.
- Enriched software pool and more efficient software development.
- Trends toward the internationalization of the industry and investigation of software development capabilities of developing nations centered on China and Asian-NICs to fill supply/demand gap for software.
- Interoperability (e.g., OSI-Open Software Interconnection) worldwide and various standardization of end user interfaces is seen as a trend.
- Systems integration combining and adding new technology to base products of medium to small size manufacturers.
- Distribution of information services (value added, beyond telecommunication and networking).
- Multiple media terminals.
- "Information Literacy", training, and education for the general population.
- Increasing dependence on information industry implies improvements in security, auditability, and reliability (non-stop).
- Diversification of information services (database provider) which the information industry (database distributor) can provide.
- Promotion of information technology in nonmetropolitan areas.

In the U.S., government and industry have formed organizations with software development technology activities such as: the DoD Software Engineering Institute (SEI) at Carnegie Mellon University; the National Science Foundation Software Engineering Research Center (NSF SERC) with Purdue University and University of Florida; Microelectronics and Computer Technology Corporation (MCC); the Software Productivity Consortium (SPC); Open Software Foundation (OSF).

But none of these have the kind of nationally coordinated focus, goal setting, and funding which MITI and IPA provide in Japan.

Reducing to Practice Developments in the West

> You can observe a lot by watching. . . .
>   —attributed to Yogi Berra

In the private sector, the Japanese Computer Manufacturers have been closely following the development of programming, design, and testing methodologies in the West.

The JCMs have experimented with various methodologies and tools since the 1970's. They have been following developments in software engineering methodologies since the mid-1970's (structured programming, top-down design, inspections, quality control circles, etc.). In the late 1970's and early 1980's, they began to institutionalize these methodologies and began building various tool sets to automate or control various software development tasks (library control, graphics for low level design, reusable parts, test coverage, etc.). They have methodically applied the quality control techniques which were so successful in manufacturing settings to software development, employed statistical methods for analyzing costs and testing, promoted widespread usage of quality control techniques, and utilized test coverage tools.

The JTECH Panel report on Computer Science, prepared by SAIC, for the U.S. Department of Commerce indicated that Japan was behind in basic software research and advanced software development, but even with and gaining on the U.S. in delivering product software. However, a variety of published journal and conference papers,[4-11] indicate that research and advanced development on a variety of software development technologies is starting to show progress. The JCMs began commercially offering a variety of mainframe "CASE" application development support systems for COBOL which use graphics, data dictionaries and support reuse and code generation. They continue to experiment with different requirements, high level design, and low level design languages and notations and hypertext for documentation. Many JCMs use "integrated development support environments" on mainframes for internal development which have graphical design and coding interfaces. Some of the systems have the concept of "reusable software parts" and have facilities for building up libraries of these parts. Experimentation with artificial intelligence and knowledge based expert systems approaches are also being reported as assists for software development and testing.

In 1985, a U.S. Department of Commerce report summarized in *IEEE Computer*[12] described the JCM focus on software development as follows:

> The Japanese are apparently ahead of U.S. firms in making improvements to existing technologies from the U.S. and Europe, and in incorporating these into highly marketable products. The Japanese have also made impressive gains in the development of software tools and have encouraged their widespread use to boost productivity. Both the Japanese government and the leading computing manufacturers began investing in the automation of the software development process nearly seven years ago.

In the same year, MITI and IPA embarked on the five-year SIGMA project (Software Industrial Generator and Maintenance Aids) which, if successful, will result in an industry-wide standard, workstation based, software development platform. The published goals of SIGMA were to improve productivity by a factor of 4 and to build a machine independent, standardized development environment and a common network for exchanging programs and technical information. Those goals have led to a 1988 prototype SIGMA workstation environment with interfaces to the JCM mainframe systems. In the past three years, the JCMs with MITI guidance have systematized what they have learned and have begun deploying "integrated" development environments on mainframes, training programmers, and beginning to standardize on and use the UNIX-derived SIGMA workstation system.

About 177 companies are now involved in SIGMA. Systems overview and recent status on SIGMA has been published by the IPA.[13-15] Common tools, business application tools, and scientific tools are finishing implementation and undergoing prototype usage. Several SIGMA centers for networking and database have been identified. The plan to begin using the SIGMA software and workstations in 50 companies starting in early 1988 as a trial before general production usage in mid-1988 has kept on schedule.

While there does not appear to have been any "breakthrough" technology apparent in SIGMA and other reports from Japan, there has been the steady assimilation of published work in the West and exploration/adaptation in Japan, followed by efforts to bring the best available techniques and tools into practical usage with a heavy emphasis on quality control.

Recently, MITI launched a task force for "FRIEND 21" (FutuRe Information Environment Development for the 21st century) aimed at developing an advanced technology with strong emphasis on user friendliness: Japanese language, graphics and advanced interfaces. This is a new six year effort, begun in FY 1988.

Similar themes are also apparent in the West:

- Promoting various methodologies including: structured programming, top-down design, data flow design, enterprise analysis, inspections and reviews, etc.
- Concern about "up stream" requirements and design activities

- Touting higher level languages for design and programming
- Applying tools and programming language improvements to commercial application programming
  - Developing software development environments and "integrated" tools
  - Using workstation and exploiting graphical notations for design and programming
  - Emphasizing reuse technologies for productivity
  - Exploring Artificial Intelligence (AI) for traditional software development
  - Forming national or joint venture research organizations focusing on software technologies

Yet there has not been an equivalent, coordinated, national investment in technology and training with the goals to bring advanced software development technology into widespread usage in the U.S. What we are seeing now is the logical continuation of what was reported five years ago in the work done by University of South Florida[16] and the IBM-sponsored project at the University of Maryland.[17]

If the published reports are true, the Japanese computer manufacturers and Japanese computer science research community appear to be continuing a steady advance on a broad set of software issues and deployment and usage of software development methodologies, tools and workstations.

Impressive claims for quality and significantly improved productivity based on software engineering methodologies, quality control, and tool environments appear throughout the published Japanese literature. The West can dispute the numbers or the counting methodology, but we cannot dispute the Japanese commitment and belief that what they are using does make a significant difference.

Computer Science Literacy

Japan's basic literacy rate has been reported as high as 99.8%. The percentage of the population completing Japanese secondary school (which has higher standards than U.S. schools) is far greater than Japan's closest educational rivals, Canada and the United States.[18] MITI is well aware of the shortage of trained Japanese software developers and has begun laying the groundwork for new education programs in Japan with specialized universities.

Japan currently has over 430,000 programmers and projects a shortage of over 970,000 by 2000. MITI's Council on the Structure of Industry expects software to grow from 1.05% of Japan's GNP (approx. $23B) to 3.97% (estimated $233B) by the year 2000 with 2.15M software engineers according to published reports.[19]

To address the projected shortage, MITI is reportedly planning to

- establish a central university for information processing for research and development on software technology education methods and instructor training,
- establish local universities for information and processing,
- continue development of Computer Aided Instruction (CAI) systems,
- develop a central data base to integrate a number of previous independently built information data bases,
- install an online network linking all software subcontractors, and
- establish a council to nominate model technical colleges to introduce an advanced software engineering curriculum.

In addition, MITI is also interested in software joint ventures with China and other Asian-NICs to fill the gap in skills at home. MITI also drafted a bill aimed at delocalizing software industries which are currently clustered in the Tokyo region. The bill provides that the government would build basic facilities and provide tax and financial incentives to lure companies away from Tokyo. Software industrial centers would be constructed at 20 locations across Japan.

It is also reported that MITI was planning to establish a "Research Institute of Software

Engineering" where major information services companies will develop technologies to improve software productivity, reliability, and technology transfer to Asian countries (trainees from these countries will be part of the institute).

Directions

A U.S. national agenda to aggressively promote development of software technology and software engineering education has not materialized from Congress, DARPA, NSF, or the DoD Software Engineering Institute at Carnegie-Mellon University. The U.S. has nothing comparable to the MITI guided initiatives. What actions have been taken in the Computer Science arena based on the recommendations of the Japan Technology (JTECH) assessment?[3] Those studies were prepared for the purpose of aiding the U.S. response to Japan's technological challenge. A much wider, coordinated, national agenda on advanced software development technology and computer science literacy is needed.

Both the U.S. Government and the private sector must make the difficult decision to commit to invest and modernize our software development methods, education, tools, and deployed workstation technology soon, if we expect to be able to compete effectively in the marketplaces which JCM developed complex systems software will be entering world-wide in the next decade.

References

1. Larry Rosenthal (Associated Press), "Top competitor? It's Japan, Inc. IBM chief says," Poughkeepsie Journal, September 20, (1988).
2. ____ "Nihon Jyohou Sangyo Shimbun," the Japan Information Industry Newspaper, April 7, 1987.
3. Science Applications International Corporation, Japanese Technology Assessment: Computer Science, Opto- and Microelectronics, Mechatronics, Biotechnology, pp. 23-88, Noyes Data corporation, Park Ridge, N.J., 1986.
4. D. Tajima and T. Matsubara, "Inside the Japanese Software Industry," IEEE Computer, 17 No. 3, 34-43, March (1984).
5. ____, "Six JCM's Strategies for the 1990's," pp. 55-144. Nikkei Computer, special issue, October 13, 1986.
6. ____, "Proceedings of the 32nd National Conference of the Information Processing Society of Japan," Information Processing Society of Japan, March, 1986.
7. ____, "Proceedings of the 33rd National Conference of the Information Processing Society of Japan", Information Processing Society of Japan, October, 1986.
8. ____, "Proceedings of the 34th National Conference of the Information Processing Society of Japan," Information Processing Society of Japan, April, 1987.
9. ____, "Proceedings of the 35th National Conference of the Information Processing Society of Japan," Information Processing Society of Japan, September, 1987.
10. ____, "Proceedings of the 36th National Conference of the Information Processing Society of Japan," Information Processing Society of Japan, April, 1988.
11. ____, "Proceedings of the 37th National Conference of the Information Processing Society of Japan," Information Processing Society of Japan, September, 1988.
12. W. Myers, "Assessment of the Competitiveness of the U.S. Software Industry," IEEE Computer, 18, No. 3, 81-92, March (1985).
13. ____, "Second SIGMA Symposium Text," Information Technology Promotion Agency SIGMA System Development Office, June, 1986.
14. ____, "SIGMA Project Report," Information Technology Promotion Agency SIGMA System Development Office, March, 1988.
15. ____, "What's New SIGMA," Information Technology Promotion Agency SIGMA System Development Office, September, 1988.

16. K.H. Kim, "A Look at Japan's Development of Software Engineering Technology," IEEE Computer, 16, No. 5, 26-37, May (1983).
17. Marvin V. Zelkowitz, Raymond T. Yeh, Richard G. Hamlet, John D. Gannon, and Victor R. Basili, "Software Engineering Practices in the U.S. and Japan," IEEE Computer, 17, No. 6, 57-66, June (1984).
18. Jack Baranson, The Japanese Challenge to U.S. Industry, p. xii, Lexington Books, DC. Heath and Company, Lexington, MA., 1981.
19. ___, "Asahi Shimbun," Asahi Newspaper, April 21, 1987.

SUSAN L. GERHART

Complexity, Multiple Paradigms, and Analysis

This position statement first proposes a theory about the origins of complexity in software systems and then discusses some responses to the problem: address the complexity of the world reflected in the system as well as the internal complexity of the system; investigate multi-paradigm approaches as a wide-sweeping strategy; establish a baseline of software engineering knowledge and build up to it; and stimulate a transition to computation-intensive software production. For the last, I propose a novel cultural experiment: a national network-based analysis game with the objective of demonstrating a fully understood software system within 3 years, where the rules of the game drive a new production paradigm.

Observations on Complex Systems

What makes complex systems complex? Is complexity inherent when software is the focal point of the system? How can we characterize the complexity of software systems? Can we identify avoidable and unavoidable kinds of complexity? Looking at systems from a broad perspective, we see several ways in which they may be complex:

- Structure—Subsystems, modules, macros, down to statements and expressions
- Behavior—Observable activity of a system
- Function—Transformations on components of the state
- Process—Flow of control
- Reactivity—Events to which the system must respond
- Timing—Constraints on response times
- State—Persistent and transient data with associated consistency and correctness invariants
- Application—Requirements from the system context
- Recovery of state and continuation of reactivity
- Security of state from destruction or unwanted inspection
- Safety from catastrophic external or internal events
- Interfaces with users and other systems
- Operations which maintain the state and continuity of the system
- Development Environment—People and processes producing the code
- Design and implementation
- Documentation and training
- Verification, validation, and certification

In most complex systems no one of the above is particularly simple. Even a small running system may be quite complex and ultimately large when all the development, operational, and interface aspects are considered. A complex software systems is much more than just code.

Software inherits the complexity of the world in which it operates, coming from hardware, users, and technological progress. By nature, software always will be pushed as far as possible to supply flexibility, variability, extensibility, and evolvability. Thus, maybe we should not look at complexity as a property of software systems but primarily as a property of their environments. The software for a tax code cannot be less simple than the tax code itself, a user interface is often meant to allow the user to mess with the system's state, and most environments have some users and accidents that are hostile to computer systems. A software system often is attacking what Rittel calls a "wicked problem", one where the advance of the system changes the environment so that additional problems are created as the original one appears to be solved (although it often wasn't the real problem, anyway).

A simple example is an institutional calendar system, a shared list of events that everybody should know about. The management of calendar data is not hard, nor is a pleasant interface, though the complexity of each is influenced by the technology base, e.g., a standard relational data base. But the calendar operations are the killer: who puts the data in (it's not fun and it's easy to forget to do it) and when an event is canceled or changed, does the system adapt well to change? Plus, users always want to extend functionality, e.g., to schedule meeting rooms or provide personal calendar services. Everybody knows exactly what the requirements are for such a system: support *my* personal calendar habits. Soon, the calendar system becomes contentious as it intrudes on policy (who has priority for rooms?) or privacy (who stays home in the morning?). Or, it becomes more and more relied upon until the day when somebody forgets to add an important staff meeting and half the staff miss an important announcement. The opportunity for an institutional calendar system was clear, implementation was reasonably easy at first, but the system isn't only the implemented software, it's also the entire operations and the changes in environment to utilize that opportunity.

What techniques are known for controlling these various kinds of complexity? Programming languages have come a long way toward providing good structuring mechanisms and principles, but there are still few tools for evaluating the structural complexity of a system or presenting the structure in an intelligible graphical manner. Timing and reactivity are yielding to a few good real-time CASE products on the market, but the theory is still weak and the design methodology is obscure. Function and state descriptions are amenable to formal techniques that are becoming more widely used. Interfaces, especially graphical, have been stimulated by the progress in scientific visualization and the power of workstations and PCs but software engineers still lack the presentation techniques of physical system engineers or even social scientists. Though not a part of computer science, the field of systems definition (or "systems analysis"), i.e., automating existing systems and defining requirements for new ones, is well developed with widely practiced techniques. Recovery, safety, performance, and security are well established, but difficult, fields of computer science, unfortunately rather insular. Design theory is a newly recognized field and some theories about structure, capture, and use of design rationale are being explored. Operations and some aspects of development are the challenge for new ideas in process programming (processes are just another form of software). Development practices are slowly improving through internal company education programs. The coordination of technical teamwork (computer supported cooperative work) is a whole new field utilizing networks, social science, and distributed computing theory. Documentation through hypertext and multi-media training are on the horizon. And computer networks link the research and development communities so that ideas move fast and informal communication supports new forms of learning.

If the above is mainly good news, then why does the creation of a software system always end up mired in difficulty and the end system appear so unbelievably complex? I argue that this is because software reflects the complexity of the world around it and is naturally used as the manager of complexity, pushing beyond the limits of experience and often beyond the analytic capabilities of the scientific base. We know we can't predict the performance of a system or work through all the possible test cases, but those limits always tend to be disregarded as complex systems are undertaken.

In addition, there's simply an awful lot to know to build a complex system. Specialists may understand how to control complexity of some aspects of a system, but the total knowledge is beyond any individual, beyond most projects, and poorly organized. The computer scientist focuses, properly, on the theoretically based aspects of the complex systems. Software engineering branches out to incorporate process programming and system definition, but few software engineers have the specialists' knowledge for quality factors, such as performance and security. Application scientists and engineers have techniques for understanding the problems being embedded in software, but they have difficulties communicating with software engineers and computer scientists. And, because system development is still so unpredictable and the options change so frequently, managers cannot get a handle on the development or certification processes.

So, what can we do? Taking the definition of the problem as "opportunity lost" may be the wrong point of view. Realizing that software provides an opportunity to bring complexity in the world under some control may be more fruitful, e.g., eliminating ad hoc procedures, regularizing some related data base, and slowing down change.

> Total Complexity = existing environment complexity (recognized or not)
> + the internal complexity of the introduced system
> + the operational complexity of procedures for using and maintaining the system
> + the development environment complexity
> + the complexity of inducing change in the world to utilize the opportunity.

My Worst Problems with Software

First, the existence of multiple paradigms is a much bigger problem than might be expected. A paradigm—mine is logic programming—gets a big hold on one's intellect and makes the understanding of other paradigms harder. While I use an object-oriented window system, I cannot fully grasp the virtues of object-oriented programming extolled by my colleagues. They seem to see structure in a set of classes that I cannot, and I'm always looking for invariants that hold the system together that they don't miss. Inheriting from all around makes me nervous, but is supposedly trustworthy. My paradigm involves expressing relations, many of which may be computed in various input-output combinations and from sets of constraints—writing a single deterministic function seems so impoverished. I see computation as just a special, well controlled case of inferencing. Evaluating a program symbolically through successive binding of variables to concrete expressions is the most natural thing in my world, but that's not object-oriented.

While these are seemingly program level complaints, they begin to illustrate why research on software problems may have trouble reaching the scale needed—software support systems require both of these paradigms and more. And so do large complex applications. Single paradigms are the drivers of much modern computer science, and the source of much enthusiasm and talent in the work force. The lack of a unifying philosophy (when to use each) and of good techniques for combining useful paradigms for a particular problem (rather than being shoved into using only one for everything) is one challenge for computer science. It won't solve the total complexity problem but it could smooth out much of the internal complexity difficulties (with appropriate analysis capabilities).

Second, there isn't yet a baseline of knowledge possessed by either software researchers or system builders. My experience with the Wang Institute faculty impressed me that such a baseline does exist. This baseline is a way of describing the bulk of what people should have read (classic articles, . . .), practiced (design reviews, using a configuration management system, thoroughly testing a program), explored (various distinctive methods such as Jackson design and Vienna Development Method), learned the theory of (grammars, logic, FSM), and witnessed (failure to understand requirements, value of a prototype). The baseline is a shared body of knowledge so that you can explain to someone "it's like A with some parts of B". The baseline is broad, covering different views, with appreciation of the differences and complementarity of those views. The baseline provides an individual filter where some people gravitate to one or another point of view, not from lack of exposure to others but consciously from some individual preference or choice of problems to be solved. This baseline is represented in my mind by the Wang Institute curriculum, not only the knowledge covered but the skills practiced in projects.

National Problems

Software Engineering Education and Training. There certainly is need for a dramatic increase in trained software engineers. Unless this workshop finds radical new ways of producing complex software systems, there's still a large body of knowledge to be learned and the better and sooner it's learned by more people, the better the situation will be. A target of 10,000 (cumulative) trained software engineers at the level of the Wang Institute curriculum is a suitable goal for 1995. The

Software Engineering Institute and other internal industrial curricula may be able to match that, with enough resources and cooperation. A major problem is how to fit this type of education into the standard academic structure—computer science departments are refusing to expand and many wouldn't do a good job of it anyway, independent professional schools can't withstand today's short term views, and rarely will companies give up the year required of their workers. Yet having this trained corps with a known baseline might make it possible to undertake building a complex system with a realistic view of what could be accomplished and what else was needed in the way of training, tools, and management.

More Computational Support for Software Production. Software engineering practice is exceedingly non-computational, despite the abundance of cycles on the networked workstations where researchers type their programs in emacs, read their mail and boards, occasionally compile, spend hours debugging, flip off some test cases to see if the system holds together, and fool around with new interactive interfaces. Despite the occasional beneficial fallouts, this is not the path toward managing complex systems. Complex systems will never expose their complexity to graphical browsing unless there's a theory of system structure, good testing is enormously labor-intensive and unreliable, performance modeling is a lost art and monitoring tools seem to be getting worse rather than improving, safety and security analyses are black arts. Overall, we have almost no control over the qualities of the systems we build, let alone prediction of those qualities as the systems are being built.

What is needed is a massive infusion of analysis capability into routine software engineering. By analysis, I mean the ability to evaluate and predict quality of a system as it is being developed. Great strides have been made in formal methods, both the pragmatic non-mechanized specification-refinement methods pursued in Europe and the mechanical theorem proving methods being applied to security applications and hardware-up vertical proofs. Yet the primary symbolic computing capability is still lacking for using these techniques for versatile analysis, and the same is true for other qualities. Similarity extraction and merging of changes are just starting to develop as programming theory. Systems that learn from usage patterns are on the brink, based on neural net and other machine learning techniques. Graphics provides an incentive but awaits a theory of what to display. These areas share common problems: promising but underdeveloped theory and high performance computing demands.

What's holding us back? Why can't systems be thoroughly analyzed? I see three main inhibitors. First, there just aren't very many good, well known "equations" around to compute with. We need equations for change propagation, for similarity recognition, for more general symbolic forms of correctness statements, for timing, for multi-layer system structure. The equations of software are more often expressed as algorithms, than the equations of physics. But much the same is needed for software—equations that can be studied for accuracy, improved for efficiency, manipulated symbolically, approximated, solved for components, etc. I believe such equations exist—an example is the clean presentation of the "implements" relation in an abstract data type theory from which verification conditions can be generated and mechanically proved and which constrain the to-be-defined implementations of abstract operations.

Second, current software engineers are hung up with interactive interfaces, and may have forgotten—or never learned—how to manage large computations. The proof of correct implementation of a top-level of a microprocessor may take 50 hours of computer time, which seems enormous, and six months of grueling work, which seems like a lifetime for a researcher. But these proofs are mainly just symbolic evaluation of the two levels and might be amenable to non-interactive computation. And they can replace enormous amounts of testing, while also improving the semantic presentations (manuals) and subsequent use of the processors. Simulation of complex finite state machine models or specifications is possible, but not widely practiced. Many errors found during debugging could be caught by extensive static analysis, e.g., checking degenerative cases. Similarity exploration for reuse possibilities should be routine, though algorithmically intensive. We need super-greps, semantic diffs, and more lints (in UNIX parlance) plus Mathematicas for symbolic logic.

Third, there hasn't been any incentive for researchers to change. The discipline barriers are very strong—performance people and correctness people just don't talk much. The U.S. cultural mistrust of mathematics and infatuation with AI and heuristics works against a broad based change. The great advances in parallel processing have yet to be applied to software problems—where would one start? Yet, we certainly don't lack for computing power to start the transition.

Proposal: National Network-based Analysis Game

Given the cultural impasse and yet the availability of computing power, is there any way to revamp software engineering into a computational enterprise? Yes, through our national and international network culture. USENET/Arpanet/Csnet offers news groups covering all the necessary topics and unites researchers with practitioners in ways that cross cultural lines. Networks are becoming the place where people go to learn, often privately, what's going on in other fields—they are a source of continuing on-the-job, as well as pre-professional, learning. Networks also serve to spread ideas and generate enthusiasm. I'd like to propose a kind of national game played over networks. Suppose the objective were, say in 3-5 years, to have a totally predictable software system. You'd be able to ask any question about it (number of structures, uses hierarchy, state invariant, response time to a particular event, . . .) and get a reasonable answer in qualitative if not quantitative terms. You'd be able to make nontrivial changes and trace their effects, not by running or by reading code but by re-evaluating equations that produce different results. Given a pattern of usage, you'd be able to predict throughput, or given a machine timing characteristic, you could predict the length of run for a given input sequence. You'd know the flaws of the system and their exact effects.

I propose a network based experiment on a given system, not necessarily one very complex, but challenging to attain a high level of predictability. A familiar commercial system such as a hospitality system or an automated teller would be candidates. Or the experiment might take a kludged up problem most people would understand, say Monopoly or some other board game, "played" in a way where the challenges of complex systems arise. For example, the state of the system might be replicated, plays might be linked to the failures of the banking and S&L systems or to the stock market, ... Naturally, the experimental system would have interesting interfaces and querying capabilities. The real game would be the technical aspects of analyzing the system, where the experimental program was widely available and standardized, although private versions might exist. The main rule of the game would be to apply mathematical techniques, not just code reading and running. The first objective might be complete verification and/or testing to extract the logical structure of the problem and exhibit minimal test coverage. Timing might be introduced by predicting the time of a run varying the statistical characteristics of the state (how many data it keeps track of) and the consideration of alternative implementation timings. A second stage might introduce changes to a standard version requiring the players to adapt the system where the rewards were based on analytic rather than traditional approaches. Later as the program became very well understood, there might be optimization techniques applied—what's the best data structure?

While such a national challenge game might seem frivolous, there's the potential to change the software engineering culture. The hackers and the professors would be competing together or against each other. There'd be opportunity to learn about alien fields, e.g., how do those performance models work? The inertia of the research systems might yield a bit to curiosity and the challenge of really understanding this program. Enough results and new research might be proposed or transferred from other fields. The national game has the feeling for what needs to be done: discover and learn how to use analytic methods for software, open up the possibilities for large-scale computation applied to software systems, and progress from evaluating equations to solving for unknown results then to optimizing.

BARRY M. HOROWITZ

The worst problem in current software production as I view it from MITRE's vantage point is that both industry and government do not take management actions which recognize the industry's inability to efficiently develop large software packages. My suggestions beyond the obvious one of not undertaking jobs which are too large (e.g., subdividing the job over time), relate to exploring

- different approaches to development (e.g., very small team size, super quality team members, super tools and super wages, and
- different methods of customer/developer interaction during development to minimize the high degree of inefficiency currently in that process.

The most critical problems faced by industry and the nation vary with the generic type of system under development. The attached chart (Figure 1) represents my view on the problems as they affect different systems. My view on solutions is that each element on the lists must be treated, so no easy-to-describe solution exists. Over the past two or three years MITRE has helped its clients to address some of the items.

I believe that too little attention is paid to collecting and analyzing industry wide data which would help companies to direct and focus their efforts in improving their software development capabilities. For example, what is the best mix of tools, people and management procedures for a given job? What is the best planning schedule to achieve maximum productivity? When are waterfall models of development appropriate; when are spirals more appropriate? Today, relative to hardware development, the software industry lacks a proven basis for taking confident management actions on software production efforts.

How can a set of industrial data be collected and organized for use? First, such data must come from large scale production efforts where the industrial problems exist. It would be desirable to provide access to this data to universities, so that analyses can be done from a vantage point of good knowledge of state-of-the-art computer science. However, industry must be coupled into such analysis efforts in order to assure a practical orientation to the results. As a result, it would seem that a joint industry-university data collection and analysis network would be desirable. Issues of proprietary data would arise. Perhaps, a government-sponsored network limited to government software development programs could overcome this problem.

I recommend the pursuit of a joint university/government/industry venture to better understand the management of production of large scale software packages. The effort should focus on building a data base which would be the basis for analysis of alternate concepts for production. Definition of the data base and instrumenting on-going production efforts for collecting the data would be the initial efforts.

Sensor or Communication Systems	Command and Control Information System
● Skill Base	● Schedule Driven Inefficiency
● Industry Management Experience	● Requirements (size of job)
● Capital Investment Limited	● Knowledge of off-the-shelf Products
● Schedule Driven Inefficiency	● Industry Management Experience
● Government Management Experience	● Government Management Experience
● Requirements (size of job)	● Skill Base
● Knowledge of off-the-shelf Products	● Capital Investment Limited

FIGURE 1 Seven software development problems in order of importance.
SOURCE: MITRE.

BRUCE B. JOHNSON

Because of the size and the nature of Andersen Consulting's business, many of the software problems of the industry and the nation are directly reflected in our own practice. I have therefore used the two position statement opportunities to discuss two separate problems which affect the industry and Andersen Consulting alike.

The Problem of Design

According to Simon, *design* is the process of relating goals, artifact characteristics, and environment. There is broad agreement within Andersen Consulting that *design* is a major problem area. But what exactly does this mean? The problem has many facets.

Developing and retaining design skills is one facet of the problem. Many of today's most experienced systems designers grew up with the computing industry. They learned concepts incrementally as the industry became more sophisticated. Today's new entrant is faced with a mountain of complexity, often in the context of very large scale systems. How does one develop broadly based skills in this environment? The typical system development life cycle is so long that only a few people will have the opportunity to learn by repetition during a typical career.

Still another facet of the design problem is the development of conceptual skills. Many systems simply automate manual procedures. Often that is adequate. But for decision making systems, abstraction is essential. We need much better understanding of the abstraction process in order to develop conceptual skills and to devise tools which will assist with appropriate abstraction. In the absence of such tools and skills, designers fall back upon known designs whether or not appropriate.

Under today's design processes, we have limited ability to evaluate a design until late in the development process. Better, earlier evaluation will not only produce better designs, but also develop better designers. Underlying all of these issues is the lack of a clear understanding of systems and design as a process. Without clear understanding of design, developing and teaching skills and developing better tools will continue to be happenstance.

The Problems of Reuse and Integration

In today's generation of large scale systems, we have two primary means of integrating systems components: 1) loose integration by passing information through well defined interfaces and 2) design integration through sharing a common data base. The former is often unsatisfying because it erects "artificial" barriers to information integration and creates user frustration. The latter can lead to a complete redesign of an existing system each time a new functional component is to be added.

Our strongest answer to this problem today is to follow sound data-base design principles. Yet any experienced software product developer understands that a major redesign every few years is unavoidable. Nowhere is this seen more clearly than in software development tools. Because the abstract representations required to describe software specifications and designs are poorly understood today, each new tool developed is likely to have its own unique representation. Integrating the new with the current or integrating tools from two or more sources usually requires a complete redesign of both tools.

The industry needs principled strategies for design and integration which rise above the level of industry standards and competitive product strategies and appeal to the minds of system developers on first principles. Object bases are probably moving in the right direction, but do not go far enough in defining design principles or in providing adequate performance.

(I am not advocating that strategies for integration at the code or object level are the only means to achieve reuse. Indeed, code-level reuse has many inherent limitations but clearly has a place in the world.)

ANITA JONES

My worst software production problem is the same as that of most folks: To produce a new software artifact, I start typically with

- no particularly relevant building blocks,
- woefully general programming tools,
- no application specific software tools, and
- general, therefore weak, programming methodologies.

The software construction process, as well as the later maintenance process, is one of dealing with the detail of programming, not with the nuances of my application. The focus should, of course, be on the application, rather than the raw material to implement it. The resulting costs that result from misdirected focus, both the opportunity cost and expended time and funds, are exceedingly high.

But there are exceptions to this situation. They tend to come from the personal computer world in which economics dictate that the unsophisticated user absolutely must be able to build his application without recourse to expensive and scarce programming experts. The much-cited spreadsheets are one example. Documentation preparation and desktop publishing likewise qualify.

Each incorporates a set of assumptions about a problem domain and strategies for expressing information in that domain. These tools are not general; they impose quite limiting restrictions. Specificity and restrictions—and the set of assumptions about context as well as domain-related, high-leverage "operators"—go hand in hand with permitting the user to express information in terms of the application, rather than in terms of writing a program. This class of tools has not been fully exploited, particularly by the computer science community. This represents an opportunity.

HARLAN D. MILLS

Benefits of Rigorous Methods of Software Engineering in DoD Software Acquisitions

The software quality and reliability problem faced by DoD today is due primarily to the failure of contract software management and technical personnel to use rigorous methods of software engineering. What is possible and practical with rigorous methods is low or zero defect software to meet precise specifications. Getting precise specifications right is much more difficult, and can be open ended as requirements change. So rigorous methods don't solve everything, but they do bring the software defects to as low levels as desirable, including zero, in order to concentrate on precise specifications for what is needed.

The only effective way known to enforce the use of rigorous methods in software engineering is to prohibit program debugging before independent system testing and to require mathematical program verification in group inspections in place of debugging. Such independent system testing can be carried out in statistical designs to provide scientific reliability projections for the software developed.

Software engineering and computer science are new subjects, only a human generation old. For example, when civil engineering was a human generation old the right triangle was yet to be discovered. But the explosion of an entire industry without time for orderly scientific or engineering development has led to deep problems for society, of especial importance for DoD. During this industrial explosion, the initial methods of programming were necessarily heuristic and error prone. With that initial experience, errors have come to be expected in software development. Since then, rigorous and error rare methods have been discovered in computer science, but are little used in industry from lack of understanding and precedent.

As long as heuristic and error prone methods are considered acceptable by DoD, why should they be changed? As a result of this understanding, the typical state of practice in software development and maintenance by DoD contractors is far behind the state of art. This conclusion was reached by two major DoD studies in recent years, a DSB study headed by Fred Brooks (Military Software) and an SDI study headed by Danny Cohen (the Eastport Report). Caz Zraket voiced a similar conclusion as the keynote speaker at the SDS conference in Huntsville, fall of 1988.

A similar problem in a simpler form occurred in typewriting nearly a hundred years ago, also just a human generation after the introduction of the typewriter. Touch typing was discovered as a more productive and reliable way of typing, as counter intuitive as not looking at the keys while touch typing was. But how many experienced hunt and peckers of the day changed to touch typing? It was a small minority, indeed. Instead, it was new young people entering the work force over several years that finally brought touch typing into common use.

Unfortunately, it will be the same in software, but with even more difficulty because of the industrial explosion of computers and software in DoD contract work. No more than a minority of the first generation heuristic try and fixers in software today will ever learn and change to rigorous methods. It must be young people with sound software engineering education entering the work force that will bring rigorous methods into industrial use.

But even here there is a considerable hurdle and deterrent when software managers have only heuristic experience. It's not so likely that managers of typing pools would have demanded that new people "look at the keys while you type, like I do." But software managers with only heuristic experience and large project responsibilities are likely to direct that "since we'll have a lot of debugging to do, I want you to start coding right away", and continue to be right with a self fulfilling prophecy, while unwittingly preventing the use of rigorous methods.

As noted, there is a simple way to hasten the state of contract practice toward the state of art, that sounds more drastic at first hearing than it really is—prohibit program debugging in contract software development, and require the use of rigorous methods of mathematical program verification with group inspections in place of debugging. By all means subject software to system testing by independent teams against the precise specifications of user requirements before acceptance and release. Indeed, conduct the system testing within a statistical design to permit scientific reliability projections of the software.

Program debugging is the counter productive sacred cow of this first human generation of software development. More time is spent in debugging programs today than in writing them. Private debugging hides many marginal people in software development. It is false economics to "let the machines find the errors" in software development, even though machines are getting cheaper and people dearer. Machines can find errors of syntax, but cannot find the errors of logic that finally persist in software developed by first generation heuristic, error prone methods.

Doing without program debugging is surprisingly easy for people who know how to verify programs mathematically. People still make errors of mathematical fallibility, but such errors have been found to be much easier to discover by testing than are errors of debugging. Caz Zraket mentioned in his Huntsville talk that software today, after all the debugging and testing, will typically have 1-3 errors/KLOC. But mathematical verification can provide software for statistical testing that start at 1-3 errors/KLOC, not end there, and go well below Zraket's goal of 0.1-0.3 errors/KLOC, with statistical testing that produces scientific reliability certifications. Errors of mathematical fallibility are much easier to find and fix than are errors of debugging.

Another sacred cow of this first human generation of software engineering is coverage testing. It is well known that coverage testing can reach 100% with many errors still remaining in the code. But it is not so well known that fixing errors found in usage representative statistical testing can be 30 times as effective in increasing times between failures than fixing errors from coverage testing. An Appendix gives the evidence.

Quality must be designed, not tested, into software products. It can be no better than the qualifications of the software engineers that produce it. In this first generation, people become software engineers in three day courses without examinations. It must become a subject of a four year university curriculum with many examinations. Universities are part way there. Many computer science curricula have courses in software engineering, much as a physics curriculum might have a course in electrical engineering. But software engineering needs a curriculum, not simply a course, just as electrical engineering has today. Moving from debugging to no debugging before independent testing is a necessity for getting out of today's software morass, and will help define a curriculum, not just a course, for society and the industry.

The Cleanroom Software Engineering process develops software with no program debugging before statistical system testing. It has been used to produce commercial software products, and a version of the HH60 helicopter flight control program. It is described and discussed in the following papers:

    1. P. A. Currit, M. Dyer and H. D. Mills, "Certifying the Reliability of Software", IEEE Transactions on Software Engineering, Vol. SE-12, No. 1, January 1986.

    2. R. C. Linger and H. D. Mills, "A Case Study in Cleanroom Software Engineering: The IBM COBOL Structuring Facility", Proceedings of IEEE Compsac 88, October 1988.

    3. H. D. Mills, M. Dyer and R. C. Linger, "Cleanroom Software Engineering", IEEE Software, September 1987.

Appendix
New Understandings in Software Testing
The Power of Usage Testing over Coverage Testing*

The insights and data of Ed Adams** in the analysis of software testing, and the differences

---

*Harlan D. Mills, Information Systems Institute, University of Florida.
**Adams, E. N., Minimizing Cost Impact of Software Defects, IBM Research Division, Report RC 8228, 1980.

TABLE 1 Distributions of Errors (in %) Among Mean Time to Failure (MTTF) Classes

Product	MTTF in K months							
	60	19	6	1.9	0.6	0.19	0.06	0.019
1	34.2	28.8	17.8	10.3	5.0	2.1	1.2	0.7
2	34.2	28.0	18.2	9.7	4.5	3.2	1.5	0.7
3	33.7	28.5	18.0	8.7	6.5	2.8	1.4	0.4
4	34.2	28.5	18.7	11.9	4.4	2.0	0.3	0.1
5	34.2	28.5	18.4	9.4	4.4	2.9	1.4	0.7
6	32.0	28.2	20.1	11.5	5.0	2.1	0.8	0.3
7	34.0	28.5	18.5	9.9	4.5	2.7	1.4	0.6
8	31.9	27.1	18.4	11.1	6.5	2.7	1.4	1.1
9	31.2	27.6	20.4	12.8	5.6	1.9	0.5	0.0

between software errors and failures, give entirely new understandings in software testing. Since Adams has discovered an amazingly wide spectrum in failure rates for software errors, it is no longer sensible to treat errors as homogeneous objects to find and fix. Finding and fixing errors with high failure rates produces much more reliable software than finding and fixing just any errors, which may have average or low failure rates.

The major surprise in Adams' data is the relative power of finding and fixing errors in usage testing over coverage testing, a factor of 30 in reducing failure rates. An analysis of Adams' data shows that finding and fixing an error causing a failure in representative usage testing increases the mean time to the next failure 30 times as much as finding and fixing an error in coverage testing. That factor of 30 seems incredible until the facts are worked out from Adams' data. But it explains many anecdotes about experiences in testing. In one such experience, an operating system development group, using coverage testing in a major revision, was finding mean time to abends in seconds for weeks. It reluctantly allowed users tapes in one weekend, and on fixing those errors, found the mean time to abends jumped literally from seconds to minutes.

The Adams data are given in Table 1. They describe distributions of failure rates in 9 major IBM software products. The 9 IBM products include operating systems, programming language compilers, and data base systems. The uniformity of the failure rate distributions across these different kinds of products is truly amazing.

What Adams found was that errors in the 9 major IBM software products had very similar distributions of mean times to next failure (MTTF) spread over 4 orders of magnitude from 19 months to 5000 years (60 K months), with about a third of the errors having an MTTF of 5000 years, and about 1% having an MTTF of 19 months.

With such a spread in the MTTF spread, it is easy to see, right off, that coverage testing will find the very low failure rate errors a third of the time with practically no effect on the MTTF from the fix, whereas usage testing will find many more of the high failure rate errors with much greater effect. As noted, the numbers work out that the usage found fix will increase the MTTF 30 times as much, on the average, as the coverage found fix. With that kind of factor, the whole economics of testing is affected. It isn't enough simply to minimize the cost of finding errors. Errors found in usage testing are worth 30 times as much as errors found in coverage testing, so the kind of errors found needs to be factored into the economics.

Table 2 develops the data that show the relative effectiveness of a fix in usage testing and coverage testing in increasing the MTTF in each MTTF class. Table 2 develops the change in failure rates for a fix in each class, because it is the failure rates of the classes that add up to the failure rate of the product.

First, line 1, denoted M, is repeated from Table 1, namely the mean time between failures of

TABLE 2 Error Densities and Failure Densities in the MTTF Classes

Property								
M	60	19	6	1.9	0.6	0.19	0.06	0.019
ED	33.2	28.2	18.7	10.6	5.2	2.5	1.1	0.5
ED/M	0.6	1.5	3.1	5.6	8.7	13.3	18.3	26.3
FD	0.8	2.0	3.9	7.3	11.1	17.1	23.6	34.2
FD/M	0	0	1	4	18	90	393	1800

the MTTF class. Next, line 2, denoted ED (Error Density), is the average of the densities of the 9 products of Table 1, column by column, namely a typical software product. Line 3, denoted ED/M, is the contribution of each class, on the average, in reducing the failure rate by fixing the next error found by coverage testing (1/M is the failure rate of the class, ED the probability a member of the class will be found next in coverage testing, so their product, ED/M, is the expected reduction in the total failure rate from that class). Now ED/M is also proportional to the usage failure rate in each class, since failures of that rate will be distributed by just that amount. Therefore, this line 3 is normalized to add to 100% in line 4, denoted FD (Failure Density). It is interesting to observe that Error Density ED and Failure Density FD are almost reverse distributions, Error Density about a third at the high end of MTTFs and Failure Density about a third at the low end of MTTFs. Finally, line 5, denoted FD/M, is the contribution of each class, on the average, in reducing the failure rate by fixing the next error found by usage testing.

The sums of the two lines ED/M and FD/M turn out to be proportional to the decrease in failure rate from the respective fixes of errors found by coverage testing and usage testing. Their sums are 77.3 and 2306, with a ratio of 30 between them. That is the basis for the statement of their relative worths in increasing MTTF. It seems incredible, but that is the number!

To see that in more detail, consider, first, the relative decreases in failure rate R in the two cases:

Fix next error from coverage testing
$R \rightarrow R - $ (sum of ED/M values)/(errors remaining)
$= R - 77.3/E$

Fix next error from usage testing
$R \rightarrow R - $ (sum of FD/M values)/(errors remaining)
$= R - 2306/E$

Second, the increase in MTTF in each case will be

$$1/(R - 77.3/E) - (1/R) = 77.3/(R(ER - 77.3))$$

and

$$1/(R - 2306/E) - (1/R) = 2306/(R(ER - 2306))$$

In these expressions, the numerator values 77.3 and 2306 dominate, and the denominators are nearly equal when ER is much larger than either 77.3 or 2306 (either 77.3/ER or 2306/ER is the fraction of R reduced by the next fix and is supposed to be small in this analysis). As noted above, the ratio of these numerators is 30 to 1, in favor of the fix with usage testing.

JOHN B. MUNSON

In 1983, I was chairman of an Air Force Scientific Advisory Board study into the same issues. I must observe that virtually none of the problems we identified and made recommendations for have been solved five years later.

In addition, I will address your two questions at a "top" or generic level.

Worst Problems with Current Software Production?

Obviously a broad, multifaceted issue, let me pick two that are decisive today. They occur at each end of the development template and are the areas least researched, understood or supported by tools. They are:

1. The inability to specify adequate software requirements and the unavailability of an adequate methodology to compensate for this deficiency.

> In light of the "80/20" concept these appear to be the areas of greatest return on investment and certainly the root cause of problems in other development phases. It has been proven that when we truly understand the "problem" to be solved and the technology to be used in the solution, an on-time, within cost, high quality product will result (the issue of "productivity", e.g., doing it faster and cheaper is moot at this point—our first challenge is to do it predictably).
>
> It is obvious to me that one of the major dilemmas is that while system decomposition from operational conception to program code is basically a continuous process, we have no tools or techniques (methodologies) to deal with it in an integrated continuous fashion. I believe the discontinuity we employ in our processes today totally destroys our ability to understand and control decomposition in any meaningful effective way.

2. The inability to define a cost effective, controllable, comprehensive validation testing program for finished software systems.

> We need a true pragmatic test engineering discipline. Today it is a truism that we test until out of money and time; not because we've achieved results. How do we engineer and plan (resources and time) for the most effective test program? It has to be a science but, as in many things, the gully between state-of-the-art and state-of-the-practice is from ten years to infinity (we'll never get there). As in Item 1 above, the synthesis process (code to validated, integrated system) is also continuous; yet again we deal with it using discontinuous techniques.

Most Critical Industrial/National Issue

All problems pale against the issue of chasing the leading edge of technology. Our biggest problems are associated with fielding systems at or near the state-of-the-art in basically hardware technology. We do not anticipate the future capability in our development of software methodologies. For instance, our state-of-the-practice can finally handle serial, monolithic systems quite well but our challenge is distributed, parallel, asynchronous applications for which we have little or no practical engineering principles. Ada is a perfect example of this phenomenon. Ada was perfect to solve the systems problems of the '70's and totally inadequate for the state-of-the-art systems of the '90's.

The basic issue is how do we identify and get research far enough in front of our most important issues to be effective and also how do we reduce the gap between software state-of-the-art and state-of-the-practice.

Other Issues

I have another pet "hobby horse" I would like to explore if the committee feels it's important. We have a tremendous effort and investment going on in trying to develop software development "tool sets". Yet, we have no concept of how this plethora of incompatible tools is going to be eventually standardized. It appears to me all we are doing at this point is *raising* the cost of doing business. Today, with little or no tooling, our only "overhead" cost is learning different programming languages—a relatively modest expense. If tomorrow we standardize on the Ada language but have a proliferation of tool sets (training on a full tool set is far more expensive than just a language) we have significantly increased the "overhead" cost. Obviously the maintenance costs for software systems will likewise sky rocket instead of reducing.

Further, there has been little or no thought towards how we keep the evolution and improvement of our tools upward compatible, if it's even possible. So not only will we have differing tool sets, we will also have to maintain various versions of the same generic tool set for the life span of the software built with a specific version.

I don't have an answer but I predict this frenzy of spending on developing tools will be a total waste and not the proclaimed panacea until we deal with these issues.

DOUGLAS T. ROSS

Understanding: The Key to Software

For the purposes of the Workshop on Complex Software Systems, "the software problem" has been defined to be *the opportunity cost incurred by users who cannot get the software they need when they need it, or cannot afford to procure it.* Of itself, this shows that we have made some progress since the Garmisch and Rome NATO Software Engineering Conferences (1968 and 1969), where "the software crisis" focused on a narrower view of the problems of software production — with high emphasis on mechanics and little attention to the *purpose* of software, which is to improve the lot of the ultimate *end user*. The Workshop organizers encourage us to "concentrate on the more ambitious task of *identifying opportunities which are not generally known* to the research and production communities," — but in terms that also address "those senior managers in government, business, and academe who make decisions about how much and what sort of research to fund with the R&D dollars at their disposal." This workshop wants *results*, and I agree. It's about time we faced up to what our problem really *is*, for when we, the *providers*, don't recognize the problem, our solutions are bound to (continue to) miss the mark!

Here is the opportunity, the problem, and the solution all rolled up into one — and I really *would* like some help with it, for I've struggled with it alone for over thirty years, now —

> There *is* a *rigorous science*, just waiting to be recognized and developed, which encompasses the *whole* of "the software problem", as defined, including the hardware, software, languages, devices, logic, data, knowledge, users, uses, and effectiveness, etc. for end–users, providers, enablers, commissioners, and sponsors, alike.

— but this is not generally known. Through the marvels of desktop publishing, I present my Conclusion *first* — where it properly belongs, as you will see.

Conclusion

In this brief paper I have tried to present, in concise but rigorous form, *my* contribution of an opportunity which is not generally known — **Plex**. I have done so because I take my ambiguous title for the paper very seriously. I *accept* the organizer's broadened definition of "the software problem", *including* their putting it in " " quotation marks, to give it a *name*, and I offer my *first* title

Understanding The Key to Software

as the title to this, my offering. My *second* title

Understanding : The Key to Software

provides the **Key**, itself — namely **Understanding** ! Yes! Understanding **IS** the Key to understanding the key to understanding the key to . . . Software — in the sense that includes the *sensibilities* of the *end user!* So simply

Understanding Understanding

is the *third* title, defined by the other two — and well to my liking, because many years ago I formulated as the only rational goal for my study of Plex

We must understand our understanding
of the nature of nature.

saying (perhaps a bit poetically):

> This is more than a mere play on words. It would be presumptuous if not preposterous to say "We must understand nature." Even the more reasonable goal to "understand the nature of nature", in which we would settle for studying the properties of reality without, perhaps, having any real understanding of the (theological?) purpose or deep meaning of existence, is too presumptive. In fact, most ontological studies, in whatever field they may be based, seem to suffer from this over–reaching of what seems to be our station in the scheme of things. Only when the goal is made two layers removed and only when it is personified with "we" and "our" do we arrive at a proper stance. We are, to be sure, in and of the world of nature, but quite literally, the world is what we make of it. Not what we make it, but what we make *of* it. We cannot foist our viewpoint on nature, but without a viewpoint, there can be no nature for us.

© 1989 Douglas T. Ross — Author's permission granted for any reproduction bearing this notice.

Nature itself seems hard enough to understand, for it has a habit of overturning each successive and, up to then, successful theory or science. Our understanding is itself a participant in nature, and certainly one of its least-understood aspects. Why, then, set that as the primary goal? It would indeed be presumptuous and foolhardy to approach the matter biologically, attempting to study brain and mind as a scientific exercise. But there is another path open — one that, when it is pursued, shows surprising promise and progress relative to the effort spent thus far.

In this brief essay I sketch the opening steps along this path, in the hope that others will join in the exploration. The primary style of approach is not to make a frontal (prefrontal?) attack on our understanding of understanding, but rather to assume, until forced to think otherwise, that the fundamental nature of nature must be simplicity itself — that the rich complexity that is so apparent is an artifact of sheer magnitudes. The known measurements of physics show that there are roughly the same number of powers of ten above us (to the cosmic reach) as there are below us (to the depth of sub-atomic particles). We (i.e. man and his sensory world) are in the middle of a vast scale of complexity. We will assume that that complexity is merely fantastically profligate simplicity. We will assume, until shown otherwise, that if there be a "law of nature", that there is just one law, and that it operates intact and in toto throughout this vast scale. We seek to understand our understanding of that law, and if the law is to be simplicity itself, then so also must be our understanding.

We must take nothing for granted. And I mean that exactly and literally. We must and do take the non-entity as our starting place. We adopt a posture of aggressive humility, lower our head, and step off along the path starting from nothing at all. In no way intending to play God, and always open to changing our stance and direction when forced to, nonetheless if simplicity it is to be — then there is nothing simpler than nothing. So that is where we start. Then, if we are indeed careful with our reasoning at each step, so that we truly *do* understand our understanding in toto, then whenever we encounter some aspect of the nature of nature that goes counter to that understanding, we can retrace our steps and know exactly what must be altered to proceed.

That was issued April, 1976, referencing "some views, tested and still evolving over a twenty-year period", even then.

In this current essay, I have done my best to present my most recent view of the opportunity of Plex, in the hope that it can become a proper part of the agenda for the future. It is a completely rigorous *scientific philosophy*, by now — a claim that I present in enough detail, with examples, to allow you to judge for yourself — and I feel an intolerable burden of responsibility to still be the only person in the world (to my knowledge) pursuing it, in spite of my efforts to enlist others *even as responsive readers*. I expect that the Workshop organizers, as well as the participants, also will not know what to make of my current effort, either, and will opt not to invest the time and effort to respond. But I hope at least that the editors of the final report will include my essay as a "minority report" appendix, whether or not it even is *referenced* in the report, proper, so that *some* reader *someplace* might accept the challenge to join me in this work, which I think is very important.

As to the senior-manager decision-makers: The opportunity is real, sound, productive, and ready for vigorous growth — but only if the invitation I extend to the technical community can ultimately lead to a group project of some sort. Realizing that any possible collaborators likely would be scattered world-wide, I went to the Workshop with the single-minded goal: To help to define a cohesive blending of our existing world-wide communication networks with color-graphics hypertext advances so that a *collegial community* of researchers and scholars can interactively pursue joint endeavors on any topic of interest, including Plex. I proposed that the resulting system be named "**The Worknet**", and that the word "*worknet*" have verb, adjective, and noun meanings, as in

"***All people***, not just researchers and scholars,
   can either work alone on their workstation
      to create *individual* solutions,
  or can *worknet* with others
     on *worknet* solutions
      as active reader/author *members of worknets*
    to benefit from the evolution of *team understanding*."

The point is that it is not the *network* that is important, nor even the *users* — it is ***their collaborative work*** that matters. **For *every knowledge worker***, a worknet bustling with self-renewing activity because it helps *every* participant to grow, understand, contribute, and *work better* is just what is needed.

There are many unfortunate technical obstacles to the realization of a truly universal Worknet, but they can be solved, and *should* be — quickly. The Worknet architecture must be *completely open*, so that each workgroup can supply or procure language features best suited to their topic, without compromise. Each group will need **both** *document* language **and** *comment* language (perhaps the same) to be able to probe the *meanings* of documents, interactively through the network. The *single universal design criterion* that *must not be violated* is that

> ***Comments*** on a document ***do not affect*** the ***form or meaning*** of the document in any way.

With this distinction rigorously supported, the *meaning* of *reader* comments on form or meaning or both can reliably be incorporated into a *revision* of the document by its *author* — for further circulation for commentary. Every *reader* also is an *author*; every *comment* is a *document*; and with meaning thus ***guaranteed to be preserved***, true ***team understanding*** can be evolved and expressed for any subject of interest.

The important feature not yet adequately supported (although it *could* be, with careful design and use of color) is to *graphically* portray the *referential meaning* that is to be common between an arbitrary *comment*–language expression and an arbitrary *document*–language expression to which it refers — with minimum disruption to *either* document — for *understanding* often derives from subtle features of the *form* or *"look"* of an expression in a language. E.g. ′ ′ ′ ′ ′ quotes ′ ′ in a quote quoted by ′ ′ ′ illustrates the convention that doubling a character quotes it in a quotation quoted by it — for which (perversely) the *commentary* language is the clearer expression! [Notice that if ′ ′ ′ and ′ ′ are taken to be single characters, themselves, then the example says ′ ′ self–quotes in a ′ ′ ′ –quotation, which yields the mind's–eye reading that ′ self–quotes in a ′ ′ –quotation. The natural degeneration is that   self–quotes in a ′ –quotation — which is the convention of the illustration, itself! In Plex, words and characters are the same, both being   –quotations which can quote. This aside is a typical Plex observation. Many of our standard conventions deepen, in Plex.]

Plex

> There *is* a ***rigorous science*** , just waiting to be recognized and developed, which encompasses the *whole* of "the software problem", as defined, including the hardware, software, languages, devices, logic, data, knowledge, users, uses, and effectiveness, etc. for end–users, providers, enablers, commissioners, and sponsors, alike.

All of us in the research and production communities would *hope* such a science *might* be possible, and we get glimmers, now and then, that some powerful order underlies the common patterns we sense at work in our successful efforts (and in the broken pieces of our failures).

It was from some twenty years of study of such patterns in my own work and the work of others, that I began, about ten years ago, to develop modeling methods that could capture such generality. The insights came from my successful work in language theory, software engineering, problem structuring, structured analysis, system design, and even business. Since 1959 I have called my philosophical study of the patterns of structure "Plex" (to plait or weave). To my surprise, about four years ago I discovered that the *reason* my methods worked so well was that, although I hadn't *realized* it, I was practicing precisely the standard, accepted *rigor of formal systems* — but *backwards!*

In the accepted *Formal System methodology,* two steps are involved: *first* **I**) A formal *language*, with rules of inference (or equivalence or ... , depending on the choice) is established to cover and allow formal treatment of the entire intended *area of discourse*, and *then* **II**) a *model* is attached to provide an *interpretation* — establishing the intended *meaning* of the language. The key concept is that of providing a *valuation* for the linguistic expressions, which is accomplished by providing some form of "Satisfies" predicate, linking them to the structured model. With this *completion*, linking language and model, questions of completeness and consistency can be addressed — and *that is as formal as any formal treatment gets!* I do just the *opposite*. For Plex, the model comes first, and the language is only and precisely the *minimum necessary* to express just what *shows* in the model. A sequence of models, each related to the earlier ones, builds up a rich formal language capability and a *very* deep understanding — all supported by the models.

The important point is that Plex is *not* merely *just as rigorous* as the accepted level of rigor for formal systems; Plex is *not informal* in contrast to these *formal* systems (in spite of the *seeming*–informality of the word–play inherent in Plex). The rigor and formality of Plex *is the accepted formality and rigor* — just viewed and carried out *backwards*, or in Plex terms — ***opposite but the same!***

The Methodology

"See and Say" is the name I have given to the methodology of Plex. It is related to, but different than "Show and Tell" which requires merely an appreciative (but passive) *audience*, who simply sit back and enjoy the presentation of the *performer*. The roles are *reversed* in See and Say. The *Seer* is the *performer — actively*, not passively. To begin with, the *presenter* is passive. The difference is profound: **I SHOW, *YOU* SEE, I SAY, *WE* TELL** — I.e. I merely *show* you the model, without comment. Only *after you have done your Seeing* (with no guidance or instruction of any sort from me, the *Shower*), do I Say what I *intended* you to see — and then we *both* Tell each other, back and forth, what *we now see* in what was presented, until we *arrive at a mutual agreement* about what shows and how it is expressed in language.

To make the method work, it is necessary that *only* **Picture Language Models** (PLMs) be formally shown. What is shown always is a *Picture*, first of all [0–dimensional, 1–dimensional, ... , n–dimensional, ...]. But equally important, every tiniest feature or relation that shows is a *Language element* [with meaning of its own, or (like letters and syllables) contributing to meaning of some larger picture–language construct]. Finally and most importantly, *there is no separate translation* into other terms *to obtain the meaning* that is expressed in the Picture Language, for *it is what shows* — *Modeled* by the picturing, itself. [This is the ultimate in WYSIWYG ("wizziwig") What You See Is What You Get, now so popular in desktop publishing!] The definition of *model* is crucial and very simple:

M *model*s A
if M answers questions
about A .

The answers must, of course, be *correct*, but *to the extent that any question about A is answered*, to that (limited) extent, **M models A**. Only with *both seeing and saying* matched so that *meaning is modeled* is a picture a PLM.

As to the *extent* of the questioning that determines the *modeling* of the model in the See and Say methodology — *that is entirely up to the viewer*, because of *No–Rule Seeing*:

If what you *see* satisfies the definition of "*IT*"
then what you have *found* IS <*IT*> !

[Several types of quotes are used in Plex: "It" = *name*; IT = *word*: <IT> = *meaning*: IT = *concept*; 'IT' = *sign*.] *Multiple modelings* (word and picture *puns*) *are inherent and intentional*, by the **Plex Paradigm** (from the little–known *alternate* meaning of the word: paradigm (n) **1:** Example, pattern **2:** An example of a conjugation or declension showing a *word* in *all* its inflection *forms*. [Webster's 1961]). Because of No–Rule seeing, the *scene* presented by any PLM is the *superposition* of *all possible meanings*, any one of which may be selected for study.

Modeling Anything

The reason I assert that Plex is *the* science that is needed for "the software problem" is that the *First Definition of Plex* is

Nothing doesn't exist.

and the first model of the sequence is *blank*. With no guidance, you see Nothing modeled in the PLM. But when I add my *formal saying* to that, your *seeing*, the full range

Nothing → Something → Everything = Anything

is modeled. That blank is *paradigmatically* a model of *anything at all!*

	everything relevant is *present*	
AND	nothing irrelevant is *present*	←THE **SAYING**
AND	nothing relevant is *absent*	
AND	everything irrelevant is *absent*	
	The **CLEAR MODEL**	THE ↔ MIND'S–EYE **SEEN** ∧
		←THE **SEEING**

Notice first of all that the four lines of the **AND** conjunction arise from all possibilities of combining the three dichotomies *nothing/everything, relevant/irrelevant,* and *present/absent* within the framework established by the first line — which expresses what we desire as that which is to be *presented* to be *shown.* "Relevance" is the term used for the underlying characteristic which *all* meaning must enjoy. That which is *ir*relevant is not worth speaking about. Therefore that first line says that I present to you a PLM of *all* that is worth speaking about. By definition, nothing is to be left out.

The remaining three lines completely spell that out, leaving nothing to chance! The first three lines, conjoined, confirm what I said, and the fourth line confirms that confirmation! There can be no question about it. As long as we stick to *only relevant subjects*, each is paradigmatically present in the showing. It *also* should be clear *why* the Clear Model, thus defined and shown, *is clear!* Quite simply, it is because *no contrast can show! Only* everything relevant is present, except for that "irrelevant nothing", which (being *both* irrelevant *and* Nothing) can't possibly contribute to *any* meaningful seeing. *To have a pattern requires a background.* In this case there *is* no background, so no pattern can be discerned — no matter *what* is being modeled. Their models *all look precisely the same* — **the Clear Model!** It shows them all *superimposed*, all at once — as one!

Just as with other formal systems when they are put to *use*, logically consistent (i.e. rule–obeying) *derivations* are the order of the day in Picture Language Modeling. Once agreement has been reached, the see+say=modeling cannot be retracted from the mind's–eye seeing of either party, and it becomes a permanent part of their shared *mindset*. This is particularly true for the Clear Model, for in a very real sense *it is the light by which all seeing is done*, in Plex. Each possibility is *modeled by its own unique color*, and superimposed all together, *the white light of clearness, itself, is seen!* For any *portion* of this spectrum, *some* completely uniform color is seen.

No color can not be seen!

This, itself, is a *word–only PLM*, with paradigmatic punny meanings, left here as an exercise for the reader. Like all PLMs, it arises from the Clear Model by crucial final steps, which I here will only describe verbally. [Elsewhere they are PLMed in detail.]

The Clear Model becomes *marked* by another agreed–upon formal Saying which uses the idea and notation of < >–*quoted semantic reference*. Being an *opposite* viewing of the Clear Model, word order is *swapped*, as well. The *total epistemology of Plex* is that

Only that which is *known by definition*
is *Known* — by definition.

Semantics concerns *meaning*, and hence *relevance*. In order to ensure the support of meaning, for the new Saying <irrelevant everything> is *banished*, by definition, in order to *realize absence*, and <relevant nothing> is allowed to be *present*, where it *cancels* with the <irrelevant nothing>, already *present*, yielding <nothing> along with the **<relevant everything>** — which thereby is *isolated* (but still looks *blank*, because the <nothing> doesn't show). That is just *one* of the modeled meanings, however. Superimposed with it is *another* seeing (for the same saying) in which *contrast can and does show*, for with both <relevant everything> and <relevant nothing> *present*, <relevant something> is **Exactly Defined** [a Plex technical term] *between* them! This is the *mark*, which is non–Nothing and non–blank. Notice that the <irrelevant nothing> *also* still is *present* in this seeing, so the **Marked Model** shows *only relevance* (as *all except the banished* <irrelevant everything>) in a *background sea of irrelevance!* — which *doesn't show* because it is Nothing! In fact, because the **<relevant nothing>** that is *present* (defining the mark) *also* is Nothing, this is the *same isolation of* <relevant everything>, *made visible by the mark!* That is what is different about the *scene that is presented to be seen.*

What I have described is what I have (PLM–)*shown* to you for your *mind's–eye seeing*. You *know* that that *mark* is there to be seen, even though you cannot yet physically *see* it, in spite of its known *visibility*. The *reason* the Marked Model can only be *known* (but still cannot be seen) is that it is the *superposition* of the <isolated <relevant everything>> seeing *with* the <sea of irrelevance <relevant everything>> seeing — and they *contradict* each other, because they *compete* over the <relevant nothing> whose presence arose from the *relevance–only* mindset established by definition. If it is absorbed into <nothing> for the isolation, <relevant nothing> cannot Exactly Define the mark, and *vice versa*. This is why the Marked Model *must* be seen as it is *known* to be — a *superposition* (denoted in Plex by "*with*") rather than a *composition* (denoted by "*and*"). Only in the Clear Model (with its four–way conjunctive completeness) do superposition and composition *coincide*. The Marked Model mindset destroys the composition possibility, leaving only the superposition.

So far *only* the *Showing* that *precedes* the *Seeing* of *See and Say* has been PLMed. To *realize* (pun!') the Seeing, requires a *further change of mindset*, making *use* of your knowledge, thereby making *real* the *meaning* of *all three relevants* that are known to be *present* as non–banished. When this is done, what you *actually* will See will be the **Model**, itself — *not* Clear, *not* Marked, but (by definition) *ready for your See–and–Say Seeing* to similarly be PLMed.

Just as the Marked Model was an *opposite* seeing of the *Clear* Model, this new Model is an *opposite* seeing of the *Marked* Model. By a definition–only change of mindset, but no change in the picturing of the PLM, the two seeings of the Marked Model *are composed*, contrary to the old mindset. The interesting consequence is that all *modeled meaning* is forced *out* of the Model into the *mind of the Seer!* — for the Model has only the capacity to be *seen*. [Its beauty is (only) in the (mind's–)eye of the beholder!] While the <relevant everything> stays fixed, a triple *swap* of meanings establishes the new mindset, as follows:

<irrelevant nothing> → <relevant nothing> → < relevant something> → < mindset>

so that the *mindset* now supplies the <relevant something>, while the Model is the

<irrelevant nothing> + <<relevant nothing> *boundary*> + <relevant everything>

composition of the <<*relevant nothing*> *boundary*> of <*relevant everything*> in a sea of <irrelevant nothing>, i.e. the Model is a *whole* having *three parts*. In effect, the *mark–as–boundary cleaves* (separates and joins) the original <relevant everything> and <irrelevant nothing> parts that were *present* in the original Clear Model! So effectively, the *mark has been added to* the Clear Model as *insight*, by this PLMing. By definition (of "boundary"), <everything relevant> is *inside its* <relevant nothing> *boundary mark*, so we *know* that <all of relevance> is what we see PLMed in there. Its meaning *shows*, but what it *means* must be modeled by more PLMing.

Scope and Relevance of Plex

Pursuit of the deep foundations of Plex in this fashion leads inexorably to the rigorous PLMing of language, meaning, and thought, itself, at one pole, through counting (which must be defined) and all of mathematics, to the physical spacetime reality of the universe, itself, on the other. As an example of the latter, a word–only PLM which links directly to the First Definition and uses only ideas we have covered here is **The Existence PLM** (see next page). Regarding the *other* pole, it can be proved in Plex that

meaning of meaning of meaning
cannot be Nothing, because of the
impossibility of impossibility

which, in turn, is a direct consequence of the First Definition.

Many startling insights relevant to our field result, such as this question and answer regarding the *information* of Information Theory, which underlies communication:

How many *binary digits* are required
to encode *one bit*?
Answer: **3/2**,
because the value of the *half–bit* is 3/4.

— which ultimately results from the fact that in *actuality*, when you don't have something, it is *not* the case that you *have* it *but* it is Nothing — it is that you *don't have* it; whereas when you *do* have something, that is because you *don't have* what it *isn't!* Here is the definition for "not it":

Given <u><it></u>, <it>, <not it> —
only <not it> is
every meaning *other than* its name.

"It" is our name for whatever currently is relevant (<all of relevance> is <u><it></u>, initially), and a consequence of the First Definition is that

it can't not *be*

By the non–existing, non–nature of Nothingness,
> ***non–Nothing existence***,
>> i.e. non–Nothingness, itself,

is

> the unique relationship which is the relation between
>> the relation between itself and
>>> the relation between itself and
>>>> the relation between itself
>
> , i.e. the unique relationship which is
>> the relation between <
>>> the relation between <
>>>> itself and <
>>>>> the relation between <
>>>>>> itself and <
>>>>>>> the relation between <itself>>>>>>.

This is a word–only PLM which actually *models*
> that unique relationship in terms of
>> the relation between X and Y,
>>> where   X is an entity
>>> and   Y is an entity,
>> and the terms
>>> the relation
>>> and   itself
>> , which refer to the sole same entity,
>>> the relation, itself
>> , which is the sole primitive for the PLM.

It can be established that
> Nothing is the relation between itself
> — which provides the background for the PLM.

The Existence PLM

for *any* <it>. When <it> is required in order for <<u>it</u>> to be what <<u>it</u>> *is* [loosely, when its time has come!] — there <it> *is!* Time progressing forward in an expanding universe is a consequence. [— literally!, for in Plex, both the root "con–" (*with*) and "sequence" (which is non–Nothing *only* in <*reference* sequence>, where "reference" is such that "it" references <it>) are rigorously defined (as is "to define", itself)].

The *reason* that the bit has value 3/2, rather than the (perhaps–)expected value, 1, is the same reason that there only is ***reference*** *sequence*, rather than *reference* alone or *sequence* alone. In both cases, *reality* intrudes. The "extra 1/2" value quantifies the contextual *coupling* of <it> to <<u>it</u>>, when we point and declare "That's it!". Such a *reference*, to be *actual*, must persist in *spacetime* [actually in what I call "***thime***" — the foundational level where *place*–like (*there*) and *time*–like (*time*) coincide], and a fact of Plex is that ***there was no beginning***, as each <now> similarly is coupled to its <before<now>>. All follows from that First Definition: Nothing doesn't exist. — the ultimate and driving breaking of symmetry.

Appendix: The meaning of any word

Let <point> = <any word>, i.e. let "**point**" name the meaning of any one word.
Then the following propositions are to be proved (another result not generally known):

P1) Let **points** be such that, *except for **identity**,*
          they *all are **indistinguishable***.
P2) Let there **be** *only* points.
P3) Let the **world** be the *collection of all* points.
P4) **Then** *the* **identity** *of a point* is the *collection of all other* points.
P5) **And** *every* point *is the whole world*.

Note: *Given* P1 – P3, P4 *must* begin with "**Then**", and P5 is a consequence (and hence begins "**And**").
These propositions provide the Plex explanation of the Platonic Universals.

Proof that every point is the whole world. (P5)

I $n = 1$: A world of one point is the whole world.

II Assume the theorem true for $n-1$ points. ($n > 1$)
I.e. for any collection of $n-1$ points, every point is the whole world.

III To prove the theorem for n points given its truth for $n-1$ points ($n > 1$):
  a) The identity of any one point, p, in the collection is a collection of $n-1$ points, each of which is the whole world, by II.
  b) The identity of any other point, q, i.e. a point of the identity of p, is a collection of $n-1$ points, each of which is the whole world, by II.
  c) The identity of p and the identity of q are identical except that where the identity of p has q the identity of q has p.
     In any case p is the whole world by b) and q is the whole world by a).
  d) Hence both p and q are the whole world, as are all the other points (if any) in their respective identities (and shared between them).
  e) Hence all n points are the whole world.

IV For $n = 2$, I is used (via II) in IIIa and IIIb, q.e.d.

V Q.E.D. by natural induction.

NOTE: In the Fall of 1984, a non-credit Graduate Seminar on Plex was offered in the M.I.T. EE/CS Department, but soon ceased for lack of student interest. That was the first public presentation of the above 1975 proof. Because counting and the natural numbers do not exist in Plex foundations, but must be derived, the preferred proof for Plex uses the See and Say PLM methodology.

WINSTON ROYCE

The worst problem I must contend with is the inability of the software buyer, user, and builder to write a blueprint which quickly leads to a low-cost, correct product.

Some suggestions for alleviating the problem are as follows:

1. Invent a formal language for expressing the buyer, user requirements; the language should be understood by the buyer, user and builder; the language should have both a procedural and a declarative style.
2. Design exploration should be supported by low-cost, quick-turnaround experimentation.
3. High reliance on rule-based programming for most code.
4. Languages, whether for requirements, design, code or documentation, should have sufficient formalism that provable correctness is possible for eliminating most errors.
5. Highly automated explanation of the software design, code, and user instructions.
6. After the initial build changes to requirements, design, code and documentation are mostly done automatically without error.
7. Iron-fisted, certifiable product control where needed.
8. Select hardware only after the code is completed.

Industry and the nation believe that software production is best managed in the same way as large, hardware-dominated, high technology aerospace systems. The management technology arose in the mid-'50's as a response to the need for system synthesis of multi-technology systems. A one year old Defense Science Board report aptly termed it a "specify, document, then build" approach.

This approach consistently misjudges how difficult software production is and how best to spend project resources for software.

Potential solutions include:

1. Reinvention of the software development process to suit the inherent nature of computer science rather than force fitting of software production to a proven hardware method; there is probably more than one valid process.
2. Employment of adoptive process models to create needed discipline plus urgency about, and understanding of, the development process.
3. Provide economic models of the development process which help with decision making (i.e., How much front-end capital investment is right? What is the affect of scaling up a project in size? Of what value is reusability of old code?).
4. Figure out what sort of economic alliance between U.S. institutions is needed to crack this problem and then implement it.

MARY SHAW

Maybe Your Next Programming Language Shouldn't Be a Programming Language

Abstract

Software needs now strain the design limits of traditional programming languages. Modern application needs are not satisfied by traditional programming languages, which evolved in response to systems programming needs. Current programming language research focuses on incremental improvements, not on major changes to the nature of software development. But major breakthroughs are needed in two areas:

- *Non-programmers dominate modern computer use.* Low computing costs have enabled a wide spectrum of application, and end users who are not programmers need to control their own computations. Order-of-magnitude increases in service require substantial shifts of technology. Computer users are interested in results, not in programming; software must reflect this.
- *Requirements for large complex software systems exceed our production ability.* Growth of demand is greater than growth of capacity, and system requirements exceed the scope of conventional languages. Software lacks a true engineering base. Language concepts can support a design level above the algorithm/data structure level and contribute to an engineering discipline.

Programming language designers must look beyond the traditional systems programming domain and tackle problems of special-purpose software and system-level software design.

Software Needs Now Strain the Limits of Traditional Programming Languages

Modern Application Needs Are Not Satisfied by Traditional Programming Languages. As hardware costs have decreased, computers have entered an ever-increasing range of applications, but improvements in hardware cost-effectiveness have not been matched in software.

- Computers are now in widespread use in many small-scale settings where it is not possible for each end user to hire professional programmers. In this market, nonprogrammers need to describe their own computations and tailor systems to their own use.
- Computers are often embedded in large complex systems where the major issues are not algorithms, data structures and functionality, but gross system organization, performance, and integration of independently designed components into reliable systems. This requires design well above the level of statements in traditional programming languages.

Traditional programming languages were designed by and for systems programmers, and they have not responded to this broadened range of applications. Even if these languages are augmented with facilities for concurrency, database access, and so forth, they are not only—or even the best—medium for bringing computers to bear on specialized applications and very large systems. As a result, the enormous capabilities of modern computers are not being delivered effectively to the entire community of intended users.

Both delivery of computation to non-experts and system-level design would benefit from the techniques of programming language design. Current programming language research, however, often seems to proceed from an implicit assumption that the only languages of interest are the programming languages of mainstream computer science. This view ignores the computing needs of an increasingly diverse population.

Programming Languages Evolved in Response to Systems Programming Needs. Programming languages were developed in the late 1950s and 1960s to provide better notations for specifying computations. Their concepts, syntax, semantics, and primitive types supported algorithms and data structures. They were designed to solve the problems confronted by programmers and to exploit the available hardware. Their specifications emphasized computational functionality—the relation between the values of a program's inputs and its outputs—and they were quite specific about details such as the exact order of computation. Problems and models from application domains were sometimes supported, but except for scientific numerical computation and business data processing they received little significant support.

Progress in language design has often been associated with improved abstractions. Periodically, language designers recognize that a pattern, such as a code fragment, specification, or data representation, is being used regularly in the same way in different contexts. The use of such a pattern may be automated via naming, macro generation, language syntax, or consistency checking; this is the process of developing abstractions [1]. Progress of this kind has yielded higher-level abstractions for data (e.g., abstract data types), less specific control sequencing (e.g., types), extended domains (e.g., symbolic processing), and aggregation (e.g., modules). Constructs are usually selected for abstraction because they are used regularly; thus the language designer's familiarity with a domain affects the match between the language and the domain.

Current Research Activity Focuses on Incremental Improvements, Not on Major Changes. Current activity in mainstream programming language research is directed primarily at refining language support for algorithms and data structures. Major areas of interest are:

- functional and logic programming, which seek cleaner paradigms of computation;
- concurrent languages, which seek to support distributed computing; and
- wide-spectrum languages, which seek a single framework to support multiple paradigms.

There are certainly worthwhile problems in these areas. But they do not address the most pressing needs of the users of software. The nation, and ultimately the programming language research community, would benefit from the identification and pursuit of good research problems motivated by the practical problems of software production.

Non-Programmers Dominate Modern Computer Use

Low Computing Costs Have Enabled a Wide Spectrum of Applications. Computers are becoming so pervasive that it is hard for anyone to avoid being at least a casual user. Automatic banking machines, airline ticket machines, and public information servers are becoming increasingly common. Office automation systems, point-of-sale data collection, and database interactions are changing the style of business. Networks have enabled the distribution of information as a commodity. Personal computers have made computing broadly accessible. Video games have changed the nature of recreation.

Computer information services represent a substantial share of computing services used by non-programmers. The electronic services market, which is growing at rate of 28% per year, provides such information as real-time stock market quotes, demographic data, and currently breaking news. Computer processing of these data gives business a competitive edge by providing more timely information at lower cost. As an index of the potential of this market, the Knight-Ridder newspaper chain recently decided to sell eight television stations to finance its purchase of Dialog Information Services, one of about 350 on-line data services that together provide a total of 3700 databases [2]. Last year Dialog realized revenues of $98 million providing 320 databases to 91,000 subscribers.

By now the majority of actual computer use is almost certainly by non-programmers. Many of them can use closed systems—point-of-sale interfaces, canned packages, and turnkey systems—for most tasks. Some computations may be most effectively controlled by a non-programming user who is thoroughly versed in the application, especially when direct interaction with the computation is required. Also, access to information and geographically distributed services is often more important to these users than individual computations.

Even Users Who Are Not Programmers Need to Control Their Own Computations. Closed systems can provide good starting points for providing simple services. However, as users gain more experience, they often require more detailed control over the details of their computations than closed system products provide. Many users need computations specialized to their own problems but cannot afford to hire professional programmers to develop custom software. Other users need to interact directly with their computations, for example when developing interactive models for business forecasts or refining database searches based on intermediate results.

The need for non-programmers to develop their own software is not limited to the business community. Scientists who perform large numerical calculations need better ways to specify their calculations for computer execution. They want a programming language that matches the mathematical notations they already use and makes it possible for other scientists to read, understand, and check a program. One particular complaint is that conventional programming languages force programs to be organized primarily around the order in which the calculations are *performed* which does not match the logical order for these calculations to be *explained* [3]. Partial support has emerged in packages for symbolic manipulation of equations such as Macsyma (in the 1960s [4]) and more recently Mathematica [5], which also emphasizes graphical presentation.

The earliest significant response to this problem—indeed, the first strong evidence that the problem is serious—was the development of VisiCalc, the first spreadsheet. The program was developed in response to the needs of accountants; it presented information in the tabular form familiar to accountants, and it automated the tedious and error-prone task of propagating changes to dependent cells. Spreadsheets have had very little credibility in the computer science research community: they fail miserably on most of the criteria used to evaluate programming languages (computational model, generality, abstraction capabilities, data definition capabilities, readability, etc). However, the best measure of actual utility—the marketplace—gave them extremely high marks in the form of profits, enhancements, and imitators. Spreadsheets made two significant departures from the software mainstream:

- They packaged computational capability in a form that the user community already understood; they adopted an appropriate user model.
- They avoided the pitfall of excess generality; instead of serving all needs obscurely, they serve a few needs well.

The first effect was to give nonprogramming accountants direct control over their computers. In addition, the medium has proved useful to an enormous variety of users for whom writing programs had not been an effective way to deliver computation services.

Order-of-Magnitude Increases in Service Require Substantial Shifts of Technology. This shift in the definition of the programming task mirrors shifts that have taken place in other technologies. For example, in the early part of this century automobile drivers had to be mechanics as well. Many modern drivers, however, would be hard-pressed to identify a carburetor or describe its function, let alone fix one. Also in the early part of this century, telephone company estimates indicated that the use of telephones—and hence the demand for operators—was growing at such a rate that by mid-century every person in the country would have to be a telephone operator. Now, after extensive automation, almost every person in the country is a telephone operator (though not full-time): we write connection, routing and billing programs of up to 30-40 characters in absolute decimal machine language, without benefit of editors or even backspace commands.

But software is more complicated than automobiles or telephones, and the users' need to adapt it and to develop new applications is much greater. *The major current obstacle to widespread, effective exploitation of computers is the inability of end users to describe and control the computations they need—or even to appreciate the computations they could perform—without the intervention of software experts.*

Computer Users Are Interested in Results, Not in Programming; Software Must Reflect This. The chief interest of most computer users is obtaining results simply and cost-effectively. End users often understand what they want to do but have trouble expressing it in a form acceptable to their computational tools, or even in a form understandable by programmers. In order to serve the users whose main interest is the application rather than the programming task, the programming language community needs to help simplify and demystify end-user computer use. If they are applied with the needs of these users in mind, research results from user interfaces and programming languages can help.

Improved user interface design is one of the most fertile areas for contributions to computer usability. Interfaces must not only provide the correct functionality; they must also present that functionality in a way that the user can understand. Unexpected, inconsistent, or incomprehensible system behavior can make a perfectly functional system unusable.

Even when software systems have specialized functions, it is often useful to think of them as implementing specialized, application-specific programming languages [6]. Programming language design concepts can help to simplify syntax and decompose tasks into regular, consistent elements. They can also help to identify good constructs for taking advantage of improved physical interfaces such as three-dimensional and color graphics and high-resolution images. The chief risks of using ideas from language design are in succumbing to the temptations of excess generality and in assuming that the user thinks like a software designer.

A system must sustain a single user model; in language design terms this is preservation of semantic consistency. For example, non-programmers should not need to make distinctions between the command language and the application language, between editing and compilation, and so on. This integration is particularly important for distributed systems; uniformly addressable networks and seamless flow from local to remote computing are especially important.

The Macintosh made a major step toward delivering computer power to non-experts. It provides a single style of interaction, data interchange compatibility among applications, and a large (and growing) set of applications which share a direct manipulation model that seems natural to a wide class of users. This machine and its software, derived from mainstream computer science research, has both academic credibility and academic popularity. It was originally bundled with word processing and picture-making software (MacWrite and MacPaint) rather than with a programming language such as Basic. Though there was considerable skepticism in the programming community about it at the time, this decision reflected a significant shift of attitude about computers, from devices for executing users' programs to deliverers of computing services to end users.

Requirements for Large Complex Software Systems Exceed Production Ability

Growth of Demand Is Greater Than Growth of Capacity. Software costs for both development and maintenance are still largely labor-related, yet the supply of computer professionals is insufficient to meet the demand. Neither the number nor the productivity of professionals is increasing fast enough. Programmer productivity grows at a rate of 4-6% annually [7], but demand growth can be as high as 20-25% [8] (Figure 1). An annual increase in the population of programmers estimated at around 4% does little to alleviate the shortfall.

It is not uncommon for the development of a software system to get out of control. A recent survey of 600 clients of a large accounting firm showed that at least 35% have system developments that are out of control: millions of dollars over budget, years behind schedule, and less effective than promised. For example, in 1982 a major insurance company began an $8 million automation project scheduled for completion in 1987; the current estimate is for completion in 1993 at a cost of $100 million [9]. In addition to the obvious expenses of system overruns and failures, we suffer opportunity costs because some projects are not even attempted.

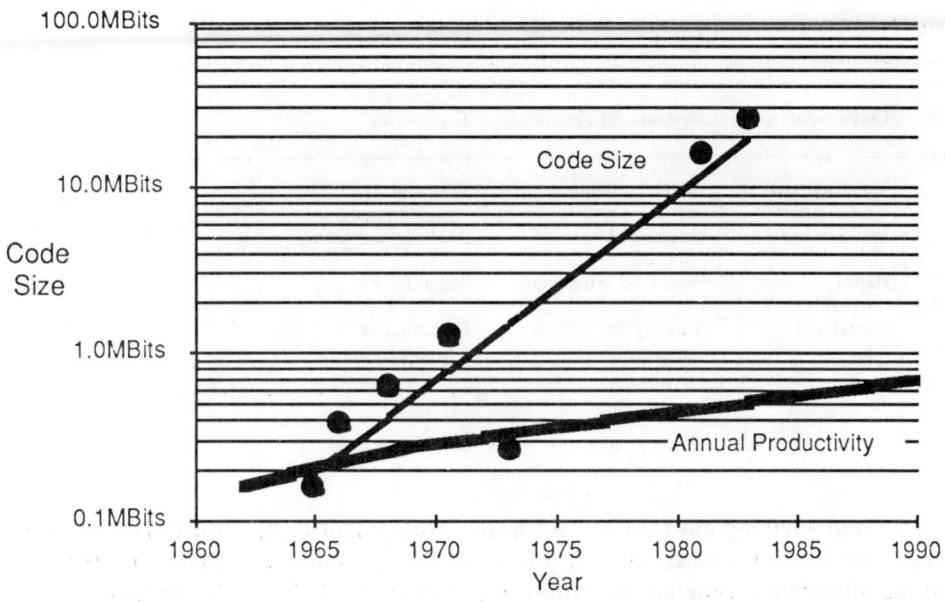

FIGURE 1 Onboard code size for manned spacecraft and annual programmer productivity.

System Requirements Exceed the Scope of Conventional Programming Languages. Modern software system products are no longer self-contained systems that simply process information, delivering results that are subject to human monitoring and, if necessary, intervention. Systems now involve responses too fast to monitor, interconnections between systems and data bases, and high requirements for reliability, safety, and security. They often control machinery or physical processes with hard real-time requirements. They must deal gracefully with incomplete and conflicting information, and their sheer scale and complexity may be so large that the implications of a design change are essentially impossible to understand.

Large complex system designs involve relations among subsystems, rather than algorithms and data structures. They require specification and prediction of properties such as space, time, throughput, reliability, security, and synchronization with external events. Subsystems often deal with long-term persistence (e.g., file systems and data bases) or distributed responsibilities (e.g., scheduling, communication) rather than with the relation between inputs and outputs. A number of techniques for specifying system organizations have been developed [10], but the programming language community has paid little more attention to them than it has to spreadsheets.

Not until the mid-1970s did programming language support extend beyond the module boundary to system-level tasks such as module interconnection specifications and configuration management [11,12]. Even now, module interconnection or system modeling languages focus on simple procedural interfaces, providing little support for connecting subsystems by data sharing, data flow, or interleaving of code. They also offer little help for taking advantage of knowledge about special properties of modules, such as the fact that if a module defines an abstract data type then its specification is an algebra and it preserves certain invariants.

In addition, large software system development requires coordination among many programmers. Conventional programming languages were designed for programmers working as individuals. They provide ways to define algorithms and data structures but not to coordinate the efforts of multiple programmers. Integrated programming environments support more efficient use of the existing tools, but they don't extend the range of the individual tools.

Software Lacks a True Engineering Base. Thus software design, unlike design in classical

TABLE 1 Engineering Evolution

	Craftsmanship	Commercial Practice	Professional Engineering
Practitioners	Virtuosos and amateurs	Skilled craftsmen	Educated professionals
Practice	Intuition and brute force	Established procedure	Analysis and theory
Progress	Haphazard and repetitive	Pragmatic refinement	Scientific
Transmission	Casual and unreliable	Training in mechanics	Education of professionals

engineering fields, is often anything but routine. Software development lacks good predictive and analytic techniques. Only in limited cases can the properties of a product be predicted from an initial design, and measurement techniques for software products are shaky. Software lacks detailed engineering handbooks in which design and implementation alternatives are cataloged along with quantitative specifications of useful properties; such handbooks are the mainstay of classical engineering practice [13,14].

Engineering disciplines evolve from craftsmanship through commercial practice to professional status. Those stages differ in significant ways (Table 1). Craftsmanship gives way to commercial practice when the significance of a product is great enough that informal production doesn't satisfy demand. At this point production, financial, and marketing skills join the craft skills to form the basis of a formal market. The needs of this market usually generate technological problems that feed an associated science; good science has often been driven by just such problems. When the science becomes mature enough to supply cost-effective solutions, it provides the basis for professional engineering practice [15,16].

Software practice is now in transition from craftsmanship to commercial practice. The phrase "software engineering" is a statement of aspiration, not a description. A scientific basis is emerging from computer science, but it takes 10-20 years for an idea to mature (consider data types, algorithms, and compiler development techniques) and the coupling between practical problems and good research ideas is weak.

Language Concepts Can Support a Design Level Above the Algorithm/Data Structure Level. Progress in programming languages is closely coupled with the development of useful abstractions and the associated analytic techniques. Each new set of abstractions suppresses some body of detail that has become more or less standardized and reduces the chance of simply writing it down wrong. Thus symbolic assemblers eliminated the need to hand-place code and data in memory; the usual control constructs of imperative languages codified some common (and error-prone) assembly-language sequences; data types and the associated checking code allow the classification of variables according to intended use; and so on. Each of these eliminated some detail and increased the conceptual size or computational leverage of the primitives used by the programmer. By doing so, it freed up energy for programmers to deal with larger problems, and thereby to discover new patterns for which to develop abstractions.

Software system design deals with higher-level constructs and different properties from conventional programming languages. Nevertheless, language concepts such as *precise semantics for primitive elements* and *combining operators*, *abstraction* (the ability to extend the language by naming a defined construct), and *closure* (the ability to use a defined construct on an equal footing with a primitive element or operator) are as important for system-level elements as for algorithms and data structures.

The major problem with developing large complex software-intensive systems is the overall organization of the system, not the implementation of the individual modules. Good abstractions are needed at this level, the *software architecture* level. Architectural styles and useful subsystem elements must be identified and classified. For example, unix pipe/filter organizations and data abstraction organizations are useful in different settings; they have different control and communication properties, and the individual elements (filters and abstract data types) are very different. What other software organizations are in common use? What other kinds of elements are used, and how are they combined? How can they be specified?

Programming Language Designers Must Look Beyond Traditional Areas. Programming languages are notations for defining and controlling computations. Conventional languages, including imperative, functional, logic, object-oriented, and wide-spectrum languages, operate at similar levels. They provide

- constructs to manipulate data elements and describe algorithms for that manipulation,
- semantics for data items, aggregates of data items, and functions to compute on these data items,
- abstraction tools for extending their vocabularies,
- type systems and other verification assistance for checking correctness, or at least consistency, and
- sometimes facilities for controlling concurrent execution.

They are mostly rooted in mathematical notations; they mostly force quite specific specification of the sequencing of operations; and they mostly proceed from assumptions about absolute correctness, not approximation or correctness with some tolerance for error or inconsistency.

The mainstream of programming language design shows little enthusiasm for user interface specification languages, constraint languages, program generators (other than compiler generators), or rule-based languages such as those used for expert systems. Generality is such a strong criterion for evaluation that programming language designers are rarely involved in command or job control languages or in special-purpose tools (e.g., structural analysis tools for civil engineers) that have rich functionality.

Programming language designers need to expand their mindset beyond classical programming, which is primarily systems programming. The notion of "programming language" should take on a larger scope, encompassing techniques, tools, and notations for specialized applications and for architectural design that require different primitives and different operations. These areas rely on the same general concepts of semantics, abstraction, specification, and correctness as traditional languages, though they will differ in detail.

Semantics need to be better tuned to specific domains of discourse; this involves support for different kinds of primitive entities, for specification of properties other than computational functionality, and for computational models that match the users' own models. Syntax needs to be made more appropriate to each user community, and support is required for nonmathematical syntax, graphics, and manipulative models. Specific areas that need work include specialized user models, system-level architectures, specification languages for program generators, visual languages, programming by successive approximation, data base interactions, and comprehensible connections to distributed systems.

The Bottom Line

The most desperate needs for new advances in software lie outside the traditional domain of programming languages. New, interesting research questions will arise from bringing language concepts to bear on these needs.

Acknowledgments

The ideas presented here have been brewing for a long time. I appreciate the support of Mobay Corporation and CMU's Computer Science Department and Software Engineering Institute. The specific stimulus to write this argument down was provided by a workshop on programming language research organized for the Office of Naval Research and advance planning for a workshop on complex system software problems organized by the Computer Science and Technology Board of the National Research Council. Norm Gibbs, Al Newell, Paul Gleichauf, Ralph London, Tom Lane, and Jim Perry provided helpful comments on various drafts.

References

[1] Mary Shaw. Abstraction techniques in modern programming languages. IEEE Software, 1, 4, October 1984, pp. 10-26.

[2] Jeff Shear. Knight-Ridder's data base blitz. Insight, 4, 44, October 31, 1988, pp. 44-45.

[3] Gina Kolata. Computing in the language of science. Science, 224, April 13, 1984, pp. 140-141.

[4] R. H. Rand. Computer Algebra in Applied Mathematics: An Introduction to MACSYMA. Pittman 1984.

[5] Stephen Wolfram. Mathematica: A System for Doing Mathematics by Computer. Addison-Wesley, 1988.

[6] Jon Bentley. Little Languages. Communications of the ACM, August 1986.

[7] Barry W. Boehm. Software Engineering Economics. Prentice-Hall 1981.

[8] James E. Tomayko. Computers in Space: The NASA Experience. Volume 18 of Allen Kent and James G. Williams, eds., The Encyclopedia of Computer Science and Technology, 1987.

[9] Jeffrey Rothfeder. It's late, costly, incompetent—but try firing a computer system, Business Week, 3078, November 7, 1988.

[10] David Marca and Clement L. McGowan. SADT: Structured Analysis and Design Technique. McGraw-Hill 1988.

[11] Frank DeRemer and Hans H. Kron. Programming-in-the-large versus programming-in-the-small. IEEE Transactions on Software Engineering, SE-2, 2, June 1976, pp. 1-13.

[12] Butler W. Lampson and Eric E. Schmidt. Organizing software in a distributed environment. Proc. SIGPLAN '83 Symposium on Programming Language Issues in Software Systems, pp. 1-13.

[13] L. S. Marks et al. Marks' Standard Handbook for Mechanical Engineers. McGraw-Hill 1987.

[14] R. H. Perry et al. Perry's Chemical Engineer's Handbook. Sixth Edition, McGraw-Hill, 1984.

[15] James Kip Finch. Engineering and Western Civilization. McGraw-Hill, 1951.

[16] Mary Shaw. Software and Some Lessons from Engineering. Manuscript in preparation.

CHARLES SIMONYI

My Worst Problem with Current Software Production

I am a development manager at Microsoft Corporation, developing language products for the microcomputer marketplace. The worst problem affecting my activity is insufficient programming productivity. In the microcomputer software business resources are ample, while the premiums on short time-to-market, on the "tightness" and on the reliability of the produced code are all high. Under these circumstances, adding extra people to projects is even less helpful that was indicated in Fred Brook's classic "Mythical Man-Month". There is also a shortage of "star" quality programmers.

As to the solutions, on the personnel front we are expending a lot of effort to search out talent in the United States and internationally. We also organized an internal training course for new hires. However, these measures will just let us continue to grow but no improvement in the rate of growth can be expected.

I think that the remedy to the productivity question with the greatest potential will come from a long-lasting, steady, and inexorable effort of making small incremental improvements to every facet of the programming process which (1) is easily mechanizable, and (2) recurs at a reasonable frequency which can be lower and lower as progress is made. I think of the Japanese approach to optimizing production lines as the pattern to imitate.

> In Hitachi's automated factory for assembling VCR chassis general purpose and special purpose robots alternate with a few manual assembly workers. The interesting point is that there was no all-encompassing uniform vision: Hitachi engineers thought that general purpose robots were too slow and too expensive for simpler tasks such as dressing shafts with lubricant or to slip a washer in its place. At the opposite extreme, a drive band which had to run in several spatial planes was best handled by human workers, even though, in principle, a robot could have been built to do the job, but such a robot would have cost too much in terms of capital, development time, and maintenance. In the middle of the task complexity spectrum general purpose robots were used. The product design was altered by the engineers to make the robots' work easier. For example, they made sure that the robots can firmly grasp the part, that the move of the robot arm through a simple arc is unimpeded, and so on. The actual product design could not be simplified because it was constrained by competitive requirements. If anything, the increase in productivity makes it possible to elaborate the design by adding difficult to implement but desirable features. For instance, front loading in VCRs is much more complex mechanically than top loading, yet consumers prefer front loading because of its convenience and because front loading units can be stacked with other hifi equipment. The point here is that simplicity is always relative to the requirements. The requirements always tend to increase in complexity, and there is nothing wrong with that.
>
> These notions have direct parallels in software production. Software complexity should be measured relative to the requirements and can be expected to increase in spite of the designer's best efforts. Frequent simple tasks should be solved by specialized means (e.g., most languages have a special symbol "+" for addition) and manual methods can be appropriate for the most complex production steps (for example hand compiling the innermost loop). This is nothing new: the issue is really the proper mix. In manufacturing, as in programming production old shops have obvious problems with reliance on manual labor and on inflexible special purpose machines, while the most modern shops overutilize general purpose equipment and fail to integrate the other approaches properly. Hitachi, in a very pragmatic way, created a new and potent cocktail from the different methods each with particular strengths and weaknesses.

I do not deny that more radical treks in the problem space and in the solution space could result in major breakthroughs and also wonder sometimes if America has the temperament to pile up the small quantitative changes in search of the qualitative changes. Yet I believe that the payoffs from the cumulative improvements will be very large. I also believe that the approach is only medium in cost and low in risk. While the usual rule of thumb is that this would indicate low payoff, I am comfortable with the paradox and blame special cultural, historical, and business circumstances for the disparity.

> I give you a few examples to illustrate the miniscule scopes of the individual improvements to software tools which can be worthwhile to make. During debugging it is often useful to find all references to a variable *foo* in a procedure. Every editor typically has some "find" command which, after the user types in "foo", will scan for and highlight the instances one by one. An improvement, for this purpose, is the ability to point to

one instance and see the highlight appear on all instances at once. This is hardly automatic programming, not even CASE, just one small step.

In the programming language we use (C) just as in practically all languages, a procedure can return only a single data item as its result. Many procedures could benefit from the ability of returning more than one data item. A trivial example is integer division which develops a remainder in addition to a quotient. Of course myriad possibilities exist for implementing the desired effect: pass a pointer to the location where the second result should go ("call by reference"), return the second result in a global variable, aggregate the results in a data structure and return the single aggregate value, and so on. An improvement can be made to the language by adding Mesa's constructors and extractors which removes the asymmetry between the first and the other results returned, resolves the programmers' quandary providing a single optimal solution to the problem, and enables focus on optimizing the preferred solution.

We will need on the order of a thousand such improvements to make an appreciable difference. It will be easy technically. It has not been done before probably because of the following non-technical problems:

1. Talented people do not get excited about incremental projects.
2. One has to have source access to all the software which is to be modified: editor, compiler, debugger, run-time, etc. Such access is rare.
3. The incremental improvements are so small that when uncertain side-effects are also considered, the net result may well be negative instead of positive. Many argue, for example, that the mere existence of something new can be so costly, in terms of training, potential errors, conceptual load on the user, or maintenance, that only profound benefits could justify it.

I consider the last argument very dangerous in that it encourages complacency and guarantees stagnation. Of course it has more than a grain of truth in it and that is where its potency comes from. My point is that if you look around in the solution space from the current state of the art and you see increasing costs in every direction, you can only conclude that you are in some local minimum. Cost hills in the solution space are obstacles to be overcome, not fenceposts for an optimal solution. One has to climb some of the cost hills to get to better solutions.

I would also like to list a few areas which are not problems at least where I work: marketing, product design, implementation methodology, testing methodology, product reliability, working environment, and management. This is not to say that these activities are either easy or well understood. For instance, we still cannot schedule software development with any accuracy, but we learned to manage the uncertainty and we can expect much smaller absolute errors (even at the same relative error) if productivity can be improved. Similarly, testing is still very unscientific and somewhat uncertain. Again, with sufficient safety factors we can achieve the required reliability at the cost of being very inefficient relative to some ideal. With greater productivity more built-in tests can be created and testing efficiency can improve. So I see productivity as the "cash" of software production which can be spent in many ways to purchase benefits where they are the most needed: faster time to market, more reliability of the product, or even greater product performance. We can get this last result by iterating and tuning the design and implementation when the higher productivity makes that affordable.

The Nation's Most Critical Problem with Current Software Production

Before coming to the workshop, I wrote that I did not know what the most critical problem is for the industry. Now, after the workshop, I still do not know which problem is the most critical, but I can list a number of serious problems with promising approaches for their solutions and comment on them. This is a small subset of the list created by the workshop and I am in general agreement with all other items on the longer list as well except that the sheer length of the list indicates to me that some of the problems may not be as critical as some of the others.

1 *Make routine tasks routine*. This is a very powerful slogan which covers a lot of territory. The implication is that many tasks which "ought" to be routine are far from routine in practice.

The workshop expressed a desire to promote the development of an Engineering Handbook to cover routine practices. I share this desire. I wonder, however, if this can be a research topic. "Routine" is a synonym for "dull" while the Handbook would have to be written by first rate talents. The whole thing boils down to this larger issue: how does society get its best minds to focus on dull problems which nonetheless have great value to society. Historically, it has always been a package deal: solve the problem and win the war, as in the Manhattan project; go to the moon, as in Apollo; and get rich, as in publishing, startups and leveraged buyouts. I am enthusiastic about the handbook but I would feel more sanguine about a "Ziff-Davis" or a "Chemical Abstracts" financing and organizing the work than NRC feeding the oxymoron "routine research".

We should also keep in mind that in some instances a routine task could be automated or eliminated altogether—the ultimate in "routinization". This is an area where my organization will be doing some work.

2. *Clean room method*. I join my colleagues in believing that software reliability and debugging costs are great problems, and that Harlan Mills' "clean room method" is an exciting new way of addressing the issues. Being high risk and high return, it is a proper research topic.

3. *Reuse*. Here we have an obvious method with a huge potential economic return, yet very much underutilized. I agree that it is an important area and it is a proper subject for research. My only caveat is this: many of the resarch proposals implicitly or explicitly assume that the lack of reuse must be due either to the insufficient information flow, or to irrational decision making ("NIH syndrome"). My experience has been that software reuse was difficult even when the information was available and the decision making rationally considered long-term benefits. To avoid disappointment, the research will have to extend beyond the "module library" concept to include:

- *Module generators recommended at the workshop as alternatives for large collections of discrete modules.* For example, instead of multiple sine routines, publish one program which inputs the requirements ("compile time parameters") and outputs the optimal sine routine for the particular purpose. I agree with this, and would only add that we need better languages for module generation. A giant list of "printf" or FORMAT statements will not do either for the writers or the users. The module creator will obviously benefit from a better paradigm. In principle, the users should not be concerned with what is inside the generator, but in practice the program may have to be at least a part of its own documentation.

- *A study of the economics of reuse.* For example Larry Bernstein pointed out that the simpler productivity measurements can create disincentives for reuse. Or, consider that the creation of reusable software is more difficult than the one-shot custom approach. The beneficiary of this extra effort is typically a different organizational or economic entity. Some sort of pricing or accounting mechanism must be used to keep the books straight and allocate credit where credit is due. This brings us to:

- *Developing metrics especially for reuse.* Assume a module of cost X with 2 potential applications. Without reuse the cost is 2X. With reuse, it is sometimes claimed, the cost will be X + 0, that is, write once and use it again free, a clear win-win proposition. This is not a realistic scenario. We need to research the cost picture: how much more expensive is it to make the code reusable? How expensive is it to use reusable code? What characterizes code for which the reuse costs are low, such as numerical routines? When are reuse costs higher than the custom development costs?

I would also like to make a second-order point. Let us call the solution to the nation's software problems the "next generation tools." It is safe to guess that these will be very complex software systems and that they will be developed by using more current tools, which connects to my response to Question #1. Scientists had to measure a lot of atomic weights before the periodic table was discovered. They had to measure an awful lot of spectral frequencies before quantum theory could be developed. We, too, should try to make the great leaps but meanwhile assiduously do our homework.

I think in the near term, the appearance of a ubiquitous programmer's individual cross development platform would greatly enhance our ability to create more, cheaper, and better quality software. By "ubiquitous" I mean many hundreds of thousands, that is, 386 OS\2 based, rather than tens of thousands, that is, workstation based systems. By "cross development" I mean that the target system would be separate from, and in general different from, the highly standardized and optimized development machine.

It would be also nice if the ubiquitous platforms used a ubiquitous language as well. Insofar as the user interface to the editor, compiler, debugger, etc., is also a language, possibly larger than a programming language, this commonality is certainly within reach with the advent of the graphical user interfaces, and in particular of the SAA standard. The computer language is a greater problem. Wide acceptance can be ensured, in general, by two means: by the fiat of a powerful organization, as was the case for Ada, or by overwhelming success in the marketplace of business and academe. Here Lotus 1-2-3 comes to mind as an example for the degree of success which might be necessary; in languages C came the closest to this. However, C and even C++ did not make a major effort to address a wider user base, and in fact takes justified pride in the substantial accomplishments in software technology which have sprung from the focus on narrow goals.

I am a believer in a major heresy. I believe that PL/1 had the *right idea*, if at the wrong time. A leading programming language should try to satisfy a very wide range of users, for example those using COBOL (forms, pictures, decimal arithmetic, mass storage access), C++ (object oriented programming, C efficiency, bit level access), SNOBOL (sting processing, pattern matching), ADA (type checking, interface checking, exception handling), Fortran (math libraries), and even Assembly language (super high efficiency, complete access to facilities). Let me just respond superficially to the most obvious objections:

1. PL/1 is terrible; PL/1 was designed to have everything; *ergo* wanting everything is terrible. Answer: Problems with PL/1 are real, but they can be expressed in terms of "lacks": PL/1 lacks efficient procedure calls, PL/1 lacks many structuring or object-oriented constructs, the PL/1 compiler lacks speed, or I lack knowledge of how to write a simple loop in PL/1. All of these problems can be solved by having "more".

2. Not having features is the essence of the benefit I am seeking. How can you satisfy that? Answer: I cannot. Most people seek the benefits which are easily (and usually) derived from not having features. Among these benefits are ease of learning, efficiency, availability, low cost. However, the same benefits can be obtained in other ways as well; typically this requires large one-time ("capital") investment which then will possibly enable new benefits. Again, the point is that simplicity should be just one means to some end, not the end in itself.

3. You cannot learn a monster language. Answer: A large piece of software (or even the portion of a large system known to a single person) is much more complex in terms of number of identifiers, number of operators, or the number of lines of documentation than a complex programming language. If some elaboration of the smaller part—the language—benefits the bigger part—the software being written in the language—we have a good tradeoff.

My feeling is that a small trend of enhancing the most promising language—C—has already started with the growing popularity of C++. I believe that this trend will continue with even larger supersets of C appearing and winning in the marketplace. I think we should encourage this trend, promote a rapprochement between the C people and the data processing professionals, and point out the dangers to those who remain locked into Ada.

WILLIAM A. WULF

The Worst Problem

The worst problem is not cost; it's not unreliability; it's not schedule slips. Rather, it's the fact that in the near future we won't be able to produce the requisite software *at all*!

Programmer productivity, measured in lines-of-code per unit time has increased 4-6% per year since the middle 60's. The amount of code required to support an application measured over the same period, has been increasing at more than 20% per year. This disparity cannot continue. Software is already the limiting factor in many areas; the situation will only get worse unless by some magic programmer productivity increases dramatically.

The Basic Problem

The problems of software development are so well articulated in Fred Brooks' article "No Silver Bullets" and the Defense Science Board Report that preceded it, that there is little that I can add. I can, however, cast them in another way that I find useful.

Software production is a craft industry. For programming, just as for carpentry or basket-weaving, every property of the final product is the result of the craftsmanship of people—its cost, its timeliness, its performance, its reliability, its understandability, its usability, and its suitability for the task.

Viewing programming as a craft explains why I am intellectually unsatisfied with "software engineering". It also explains why the software crisis, proclaimed twenty years ago, is still with us. Better management, better environments, and better tools obviously help either the carpenter or the programmer, but they do not change the fundamental nature of the activity. Not that current software engineering is wrong-headed; it's very, very important—after all, it's all we have. But we must look elsewhere for a fundamental solution.

Viewing programming as a craft also suggests the shape of that solution. We must find a way to make the bulk of programming a capital-intensive, automated activity. Here the analogy with other crafts breaks down because programming is a creative, design activity rather than a production one. However, we have numerous examples where we have achieved automation. No one writes parsers anymore; parser-generators do that. Few people write code generators any more; code generator generators do that. No one should write structured editors anymore; systems such as Teitelbaum's Synthesizer Generator can do that.

Tools such as parser generators are fundamentally different from tools such as debuggers, editors or version management systems. They embody a model of a class of application programs and capture knowledge about how to build programs for those applications; in a loose sense they are "expert systems" for building applications in a particular domain. The better ones are capable of producing better applications than the vast majority of programmers because they embody the most advanced expertise in the field. Thus they provide both enormous productivity leverage and better quality as well.

What Should We Do?

I have three suggestions—one general, long-term one, and two more specific, immediate ones.

1. Recognize that the *general* solution is *hard*! There are two implications of this:
   - We need basic, long-term research, recognizing that it won't lead to a "quick fix" (I fear that too many prior programs, such as STARS, have been sold on the promise of quick, massive returns).

- We must look for specific, special case solutions—that is, common situations (like parsers and code-generators) where automation is possible now.

I'll return to the second point below.

2. Change government procurement policy, especially DoD's! The current policy, which requires delivery of the tools used to build a product along with the product, is a strong disincentive for a company to invest in tooling. This is backwards; we should be doing everything possible to make it attractive for the private sector to invest in greater automation.

3. Measure! Ten years or so ago, IBM did a study of its largest customer's largest applications. They discovered that 60% of the code in these applications was devoted to screen management. I don't know if that's still true, and it doesn't matter. What does matter is that we (the field) don't know if it's true. Suppose it were true, or that something else equally mundane accounts for a significant fraction of the code. We might be able to literally double productivity overnight by automating that type of code production. I doubt that anything so dramatic would emerge, but it's criminal that we don't know.

Of course, committing to a program of basic research is both the most important and the most difficult to achieve. I am not sure that the software research community itself is willing to admit how hard the problem really is, and we have lost a great deal of credibility by advocating a long series of panaceas that weren't (flowcharting, documentation, time-sharing, high-level languages, structured programming, verification, ...).

It is not enough to say that we must do basic research. What research, and why? My sincere hope is that this workshop will at least begin the process of laying out a credible basic research agenda for software. To that end, let me mention just a few of my pet candidates for such an agenda:

- Mathematics of computation: I am skeptical that classical mathematics is an appropriate tool for our purposes; witness the fact that most formal specifications are as large as, as buggy as, and usually more difficult to understand than the programs they purport to specify. I don't think the problem is to make programming "more like mathematics"; it's quite the other way around.
- Languages: We have all but abandoned language research, which I think is a serious mistake—historically new languages have been the vehicle for carrying the latest/best programming concepts. I am especially disappointed that current mechanisms for abstraction are so weak. I am also disappointed in the "NewSpeak mentality" of current language orthodoxy (NewSpeak was the language Big Brother imposed in *1984*; it omitted the concepts that would allow its speakers to utter seditious thoughts [bad programs]).
- Parallelism: The emphasis of the last two decades has been on synchronization—on mechanisms for reducing the problems of parallelism to better understand sequential ones. Such a mindset will never lead to massively parallel algorithms or systems. The ideal should be parallel algorithms and systems with no synchronization at all.
- Testing and testability: Both of these have been stepchildren, and even denigrated in academia ("... make it correct in the first place...."). My experience in industry suggests that there is a great deal to be gained by (1) making testability a first order concern during design, and (2) making testing an integral part of the implementation process.

This is by no means a complete list; hopefully it will provide some fodder for thought.

ANDRES G. ZELLWEGER

Introduction

The following two position statements provide, from my perspective, some of the motivation for the recommendations that came out of the Complex Software Systems Workshop. In general, the recommendations from the workshop provide a long term attack on the problems I have outlined below. I have suggested some additional avenues that may eventually offer us solutions to the problems most critical to me. I also believe that it is important that the software community, together with the military/industrial complex, take three actions that can provide much needed near term relief to the "software problem". These are (1) education of users and builders of large software systems to teach them how to approach the joint understanding of what a system can and should do; (2) institutionalization of the current state of the art in software design and development; and (3) initiation of a joint effort by the DoD, affected civilian government agencies, and industry to solve the problem of the incompatibility between prescribed software DoD development paradigms and what, in practice, we have learned works best today.

My Most Serious Problem with Software Development

As the Corporate Chief Engineer, I am intimately concerned with CTA's ability to produce software. Our goal in the software area is precisely the goal stated in the Workshop Statement—the efficient production of quality software. To that end, we have been concentrating on improving the support infrastructure (QA, CM, software development standards, etc.), standardizing and strengthening our engineering environment and process for developing software, and developing a base of reusable software components.

For the past year, I have been conducting periodic internal reviews of all projects in the company with the primary objective of improving the quality of all the products we deliver to our customers. Interestingly enough, based on that experience, our most serious problem does not appear to be in the production process per se, rather it is in the cost and schedule increases due to changing user requirements. Despite the fact that CTA uses rigorous methods to analyze and define the computer human interface and refines the interface with rapid prototyping (both with extensive customer involvement) we still find that our customers "change their mind" about this interface, and thus also about the requirements for the system, as we go through preliminary and detailed design.

While there are many contributing factors to this phenomenon, I suspect that the primary reason for this is that neither we nor our customers have a very good idea of what they want a system to do at the outset of a development project. There is clearly a lack of understanding, but, unfortunately, in most cases, the nature of the government acquisition process and the pressures of schedules force us to begin a system design anyway. As the design process progresses, our customers become smarter about how their application could be solved (and about the capabilities of modern computer technology) and we see the classical "requirements creep". Another contributing factor, particularly on large projects that take several years to complete, is a legitimate change in user needs that impacts software requirements.

I see two complementary solutions to this problem. First, we must recognize that, in nearly all cases, a software system must change with the world around it from its conception to its demise. Software must therefore, by design, be inherently capable of evolution. We are beginning to learn how to build such software (see, for example, the FAA's "Advanced Automation System: Strategies for Future Air Traffic Control Systems" in the February 1987 issue of *Computer*), but I think we are just scratching the surface of a good solution. Second, just as the American public had to become accustomed to fast foods in order to achieve the significant breakthrough in the cost of food delivery, users of computer systems must learn that certain sacrifices need to be made to get their systems faster and for less money. Standard user interfaces, incremental delivery of capabilities, and the use of commercial packages that may not have all the bells and whistles a user would like are just a few examples of such sacrifices. Education, not only of the developers of software but also of users, is absolutely essential if we are to make progress in this area. Research into how special purpose systems can be built from standard building blocks or how tailored building blocks might be generated automatically is beginning but a great deal more is needed to make significant breakthroughs.

The Industry and Nation's Most Critical Problem with Software Production Today

The list of symptoms we hear every day, particularly in the aerospace/defense industry, is long:

- Software doesn't meet user needs.
- Software doesn't work as advertised.
- Software fails.
- Software is late.
- Software cost is more than original estimate.

At the same time, as technology advances, our appetites are growing. Systems are getting bigger and more complex. The life cycle is getting longer. Software safety is becoming more critical as we increase our dependence on computer systems.

The most critical near term problem that must be addressed if we are to alleviate some of these symptoms is the replacement (and institutionalization) of the unwieldy waterfall model with a new software development paradigm. The waterfall model and all the DoD standards (especially 1521B, 2167, and 483) served as a vehicle to let industry build and the government specify and manage large software projects. Unfortunately, the waterfall model no longer works and has not been replaced with a new model *and a set of compatible standards, development methods, and management practices*. The most recent version of 2167 has taken away many of the waterfall constraints, but offers nothing to replace the paradigm. Software developers are essentially told to "tailor". This freedom is, in some ways, an advantage for the more sophisticated developers, but places a severe burden on the government and the majority of the developers of large aerospace/defense systems. Typical questions are, What documentation should be developed?, How should we deal with project reviews, test, documentation, cost and schedule when reusable parts or prototyping is involved?, How do we implement "build a little, learn a little" and still get good documentation and coherent designs?, What should be my project milestones and when should they occur?, How do I evaluate the cost of the proposed approach and quantify the impact of the approach on risk?, and so on.

Over the past decade we (the software community) have learned a great deal about what works and what doesn't work in software development. The acceptance of Ada and with it a renewed emphasis on good software engineering practice also needs to be factored into the software development process (e.g., more design time, different testing strategies). Several paradigms that incorporate what we have learned (the Barry Boehm software spiral is perhaps the best known) have been proposed, but as a community we must now take the next step and adopt and institutionalize one or more paradigms so that the aerospace/defense industry can once again set up standardized "factories" to build software in a manner that is compatible with government specifications, standards, deliverables (documentation), and well defined schedules and review points.

The inherent need for this solution stems from the way in which the government procures its software. Perhaps a longer term (and better?) solution is possible if we change the way government goes about the software procurement and management process. I believe that a fruitful avenue of research would be the exploration of new ways of specifying and buying software and the impact of this on the way that aerospace and defense contractors could approach the development of large software systems.

ARTHUR I. ZYGIELBAUM

My Worst Problems with Software

Software development has challenged me just like other developers and managers. We have an inability to correctly and accurately predict, monitor, and control cost and schedule during the development process and the process of sustaining engineering for significant and complex software projects. Further, most software products are tied to particular groups of people and usually to one or two "gurus."

The "attacks" we have made on the problem are classic and include, in the past, creation and rigorous enforcement of software standards, the use of "standard" languages, and tools to aid in monitoring the development process. But we've discovered that the impact of any of these elements is difficult to ascertain.

The Jet Propulsion Laboratory (JPL) took strong steps four years ago to create a software resource center (SORCE) to help change the practice of software engineering at the Laboratory. Charged with the task of training managers and engineers, evaluating tools, consulting and maintaining software standards, SORCE is beginning to improve the process. JPL supports this effort at about $2M per year of internal funding. SORCE has also begun to collect software metrics and to use them to develop a "corporate" memory of success and failure.

As strong as the SORCE effort is, we still suffer from significant overruns in cost and time in trying to meet our commitments. Fred Brooks, in his paper, "There's No Silver Bullet," predicted this outcome. Brooks identified two types of software development difficulties. The first was that set of problems created in trying to improve the process. For example, a new language may reduce overall complexity over an earlier language, but will introduce new difficulties through syntax ambiguity or lack of rigor in type checking, etc. These accidental difficulties are solvable through careful design or procedure. The second class of errors is inherent in the process. Software is hard to do correctly. There are few human endeavors that are as difficult to grasp as a complex program or set of programs. The relations, processes, and purposes of the elements of a program are difficult to describe and thus difficult to use as construction elements. Creating tools, methods or magic to solve these difficulties is extremely hard.

Another symptom of the problem is an inability to discover the initial set of requirements that lead to a specification for software development. It has been said that the programmer becomes the system engineer of last resort. Being unable to completely specify the design in a closed, measurable form, we tend to leave design decisions to the last possible stage in the development process. It is difficult to manage a process when the end goal cannot be adequately described!

Underlying the difficulties I identify is the lack of an extensible scientific basis for the process called software engineering. Dr. Mary Shaw of the Software Engineering Institute and Carnegie Mellon University very articulately described this through analogy with other professional engineering disciplines. She describes three stages of evolution in a practice before it is really engineering. The first is "craft." Bridge building was a craft when first practiced. There was little regard for the cost of natural resources and the practice of building was left to "gurus" who could pass the knowledge to a few others. Extension or improvement tended to be through accident rather than through development. The second stage is "commercial." Here there is refinement of practice to a point where economic use of resources is possible. The process knowledge is more widely known, but extensions and improvements still tend to be from exercise and accident. During this stage a scientific basis for the discipline begins to evolve. For bridge building, this was the application of physics to understanding the building materials and the structures made from those materials. Eventually practice and the evolving science become joined into an engineering discipline. The scientific basis allows prediction of the process and improvement through systematic methods. Further, the scientific theories themselves are extensible which results in further process and product improvements.

In my opinion, the key for the future of software is in the development of this underlying theory. It took many hundreds of years for civil engineering. It will take decades for software. But we need to make the commitment now. Developing this theory requires experiments with programmers, engineering and management teams, and the gathering of metrics. These studies must be made both at the individual practitioner level and in "programming-in-the-large" covering groups of engineers and managers. The effort requires the use of rigorous scientific practice in the development, testing and refinement of hypothesis leading to theory.

The Complex Software Systems Workshop would be an excellent forum to provide a national focus on the need to develop a science to underlie software engineering.

Industry and National Problems with Software

Rather than the usual views on the difficulty of producing software, I would like to look at the difficulty of using software and our increasing dependence on software.

During a recent trip to Washington, I was amused and dismayed to overhear a confrontation between an irritated customer and a clerk of a large national rent-a-car chain. It seems that the customer had signed a contract specifying a particular rental rate for a car. When he returned the car, he paid for it with a credit card. It was not the credit card identified in his "preferred customer" identification. Since the agency's computer could not link the card to the customer, the rate printed on the invoice was higher than that in the original contract. The customer, correctly, I think, argued that the method of payment should not affect the rate. The rate was tied to his frequent use of the agency and to his corporate standing. The clerk said that she had no choice but to charge the rate quoted by the computer.

I was similarly amused by a recent television show where the intrepid detective told his boss that the evidence gathered was accurate and correct because they "checked it in THE computer." Computers are becoming an increasingly pervasive part of our lives. There is little that we do that is not affected or enabled by them. But as demonstrated by my examples, the computer can do more than automate a process. It can replace that process with an inaccurate representation.

Naturally, the representation is defined in software. Capturing requirements and understanding the implications of a particular software architecture are difficult. Hence the rent-a-car rules and regulations created by software difficulties. And hence the artificial increase in the cost of a product.

A recent study of students was reported wherein computer software was set to make predictable errors in simple calculations. Most of the students accepted the answers without relying on common sense. We readily assume the correctness of the computer. Computer accuracy is largely dependent on the software implementation. Errors can lead to amusement or to disaster.

I am quite sure that the reader can conjure or remember similar examples. We also need to consider errors which are induced maliciously through worms, viruses, and direct manipulation. Let me not carry this further except to note that while we are concerned with the difficulty and cost in developing software, the larger problem may be in the cost of using the software. And this cost may be in terms of money, time, property and human life.

There are several elements required to solve this problem. The first is education. That is, we must provide mechanisms to assure that operators and users of information systems understand the basic processes being automated through the system. The second is in providing adequate means and methods for identifying the requirements for the system and in deriving a correct specification for development. The third is in providing adequate testing and prototyping. The fourth, and not final, element is in developing systems which maintain the integrity of both software and information.